~Introducing Fiqh Series~
Vol.6

Introducing the Fiqh of Marriage and Divorce

(فقه النكاح و الطلاق)

Written and compiled by

SAFARUK Z. CHOWDHURY

AD-DUHA
LONDON 2009

First edition 2009

Updated Edition 2012

An educational publication from Ad-Duha London
Third Floor, 42 Fieldgate Street
London E1 1ES
E: info@duha.org.uk
W: www.duha.org.uk
T: 07891 421 925

First unpublished edition 2009

Title   : Introducing the Fiqh of Marriage and Divorce

By   : S. Z. Chowdhury

Published   : 2012

Book available in:

- Europe
- USA
- United Kingdom

www.amazon.co.uk

Ad-Duha London
Third Floor, 42 Fieldgate Street
M: 07891 421 925
E: info@duha.org.uk
W: www.duha.org.uk

Contents Page

TABLE OF ABBREVIATIONS

Art.   = article

Bk.   = book

pp.   = pages

ʾ   = the Arabic letter ع

ʿ   = the Arabic letter ء

هـ .إ   = 'end of quote' where a cited textual segment in
            Arabic ends.

s: = additional comments made by the translator

TABLE OF SYMBOLS

= *hadith* number

(…)   = contains transliteration of Arabic terms

[…]   = contains additions by the translator

… / […]   = ellipsis where a textual segment is elided and
            omitted in translation by the translator

{…}   = enclosure of a Qur'anic verse in translation

§   = section

——PART ONE

Chapter 1: Contract and Preliminaries.

Chapter 2: Key Notions.

Chapter 3: Ingredients of a Marriage.

Chapter 4: Rights and Responsibilities.

Chapter 5: Common Marriage Scenarios.

The Prophet said:

لم نَرَ للمتحابَّيْن مثل النكاح

"We do not know of anything better for two people who love one another than marriage..."
(Tirmidhi, *Sunan* [#1847])

Chapter 1: Tying the Knot and not a Noose: *Some Islamic Guidelines on Approaching Marriage"*

——— Π ———

§1. Marriage Preliminary Points

1. The Arabic word for marriage is "*nikah*" (النكاح/ root: *n / k / h*) and linguistically means: 'to have sex', 'to contract a marriage with a woman' and 'to co-mingle'.[1]
2. Marriage (*nikah*) is an emphasised *sunnah* (an act the Prophet emphatically enjoined).[2]
3. Marriage has enormous rewards and benefits.[3]

---

[1] E. W. Lane, *Arabic-English Lexicon*, Bk.I, pp.2847-2848.

[2] Ibn 'Abidin, *Radd al-Muhtar*, 3:7:

(و) يكون (سنة) مؤكدة في الأصح فيأثم بتركه ويثاب إن نوى تحصينا وولدا (حال الاعتدال) أي القدرة على وطء ومهر ونفقة ...

قوله (أي القدرة على وطء) أي الاعتدال في التوقان... وفي البحر والمراد حالة القدرة على الوطء والمهر والنفقة مع عدم الخوف من الزنا والجور وترك الفرائض والسنن فلو لم يقدر على واحد من الثلاثة أو خاف واحدا من الثلاثة أي الأخيرة فليس معتدلا فلا يكون سنة في حقه كما أفاده في البدائع ...

[3] See for example:

1. http://www.darululoom-deoband.com/english/books/nikah.htm#The%20Virtues%20and%20Rights%20of%20Marriage
2. http://www.darululoom-deoband.com/english/books/nikah.htm#The%20Virtues%20and%20Rights%20of%20Marriage
3. http://islamgreatreligion.wordpress.com/2011/03/15/marriage-in-islam-purpose-and-virtues-special-article/

4. Marriage is a serious matter in Islam.
5. Marriage is the basic unit of the social system in Islam.

§2. Finding a Spouse

There are broad guidelines from the Shariah for manner in which to seek a spouse and they are, in summary, given below:

Step 1: The right intention, sincerity and seriousness.

Step 2: Finding out information about the potential spouse through respectful means (e.g. brother, family members, friends, colleagues at work, teachers, online matrimonial sites, **or even take one's own initiative**, etc.).

Step 3: *Meet, greet and eat*! – but only in the presence of her *wali amr* (legal marriage guardian) or family.

Step 4: If there is attraction and huge potential for a marriage, then the process is taken further and if not, then there should be amicable parting.

Step 5: start again.

Related Rulings:

1. It is not permissible to date.

---

4. http://www.sunniforum.com/forum/showthread.php?32929-Importance-amp-Virtues-Of-Marriage
5. http://www.zawaj.com/14-benefits-of-marriage-in-islam/

2. It is not permissible to be intimate at any stage of the marriage process.

3. It is not permitted to be unashamed and lack modesty.

4. It is not permitted to be a fiancé in the western sense of the term.

5. It is not permitted to ask a woman to uncover when seeking a potential spouse.

6. It is not permitted to reveal past sins for a prospective spouse.

7. It is not permitted to propose to a woman who already has a proposal.

8. It is recommended to marry a virgin.

9. It is permitted to look at a woman one intends to marry[4] in her natural clothes (e.g. when she is at home) and when she is unaware.[5]

---

[4] al-Mubarakfuri, *Tuhfat al-Ahwadhi*, 4:175:

(فَإِنَّهُ) أَيْ النَّظَرَ إِلَيْهَا (أَحْرَى) أَيْ أَجْدَرُ وَأَوْلَى وَالنسب (أَنْ يُؤْدَمَ بَيْنَكُمَا) أَيْ بِأَنْ يُؤَلَّفَ وَيُوَفَّقَ بينكما قال بن الْمَلِكِ يُقَالُ أَدَمَ اللَّهُ بَيْنَكُمَا يَأْدِمُ أَيْ أَدَمَ بِالسُّكُونِ أَصْلَحَ وَأَلَّفَ وَكَذَا آدَمَ في الْفَائِقِ الْأُدْمُ وَالْإِيدَامُ الْإِصْلَاحُ وَالتَّوْفِيقُ مِنْ أُدْمِ الطَّعَامِ وَهُوَ إِصْلَاحُهُ بِالْإِدَام وَجَعْلُهُ مُوَافِقًا لِلطَّاعِمِ وَالتَّقْدِيرُ يُؤْدَمُ بِهِ فَالْجَارُّ وَالْمَجْرُورُ أُقِيمَ مَقَامَ الْفَاعِلِ ثُمَّ حُذِفَ أَوْ نُزِّلَ الْمُتَعَدِّي مَنْزِلَةَ اللَّازِمِ أَيْ يُوقَعَ الْأُدْمُ بَيْنَكُمَا يَعْنِي يَكُونُ بَيْنَكُمَا الْأُلْفَةُ وَالْمَحَبَّةُ لِأَنَّ تَزَوُّجَهَا إِذَا كَانَ بَعْدَ مَعْرِفَةٍ فَلَا يَكُونُ بَعْدَهَا غَالِبًا نَدَامَةً

Tirmidhi, *Sunan* (#1987):

حَدَّثَنَا أَحْمَدُ بْنُ مَنِيعٍ قَالَ: حَدَّثَنَا ابْنُ أَبِي زَائِدَةَ، قَالَ: حَدَّثَنِي عَاصِمُ بْنُ سُلَيْمَانَ هُوَ الْأَحْوَلُ، عَنْ بَكْرِ بْنِ عَبْدِ اللَّهِ الْمُزَنِيِّ، عَنْ الْمُغِيرَةِ بْنِ شُعْبَةَ، أَنَّهُ خَطَبَ امْرَأَةً، فَقَالَ النَّبِيُّ صَلَّى اللَّهُ عَلَيْهِ وَسَلَّمَ: «انْظُرْ إِلَيْهَا، فَإِنَّهُ أَحْرَى أَنْ يُؤْدَمَ بَيْنَكُمَا» وَفِي الْبَاب عَنْ مُحَمَّدِ بْنِ مَسْلَمَةَ، وَجَابِرٍ، وَأَبِي حُمَيْدٍ، وَأَبِي هُرَيْرَةَ، وَأَنَسٍ «هَذَا حَدِيثٌ حَسَنٌ» وَقَدْ ذَهَبَ بَعْضُ أَهْلِ الْعِلْمِ إِلَى هَذَا الْحَدِيثِ، وَقَالُوا: لَا بَأْسَ أَنْ يَنْظُرَ إِلَيْهَا مَا لَمْ يَرَ مِنْهَا مُحَرَّمًا، وَهُوَ قَوْلُ أَحْمَدَ، وَإِسْحَاقَ "، وَمَعْنَى قَوْلِهِ: «أَحْرَى أَنْ يُؤْدَمَ بَيْنَكُمَا» قَالَ: أَحْرَى أَنْ تَدُومَ الْمَوَدَّةُ بَيْنَكُمَا

[5] 'Ali al-Qari, *Mirqat al-Mafatih*, 5:2053:

10. It is permitted to marry a person for their status.
11. It is permitted to marry someone for their looks.
12. It is permitted to marry someone because they offer financial security.
13. It is permitted to use marriage websites to seek a spouse as long as Islamic guidelines of modesty, shame and seriousness are followed.
14. It is preferred to marry a devout woman (pious and God-fearing).
15. Mixed heritage marriages are permitted.
16. It is necessary to reveal any personal conditions that will affect the outcome of the marriage afterwards (e.g. illnesses, disorders, medical records, existing children, etc.).

§3. The Marriage Contract

For a marriage contract to take place, there has to be two 'parties' or 'sides' to the contract. The basic condition of the marriage contract is:

1. **An offer (*ijab*) and an acceptance (*qabul*):**

a) With words that indicate offer and acceptance;

b) In the past tense e.g. 'I have married you', 'I have accepted', etc.)[6] or present tense but not the future tense

---

(عَنْ جَابِرٍ قَالَ: قَالَ رَسُولُ اللَّهِ صَلَّى اللَّهُ عَلَيْهِ وَسَلَّمَ إِذَا خَطَبَ أَحَدُكُمُ الْمَرْأَةَ) أَيْ أَرَادَ خِطْبَتَهَا وَهِيَ بِكَسْرِ التَّاء مُقَدَّمَاتُ الْكَلَامِ فِي أَمْرِ النِّكَاحِ عَلَى الْخُطْبَةِ بِالضَّمِّ وَهِيَ الْعُقَدُ (فَإِنِ اسْتَطَاعَ أَنْ يَنْظُرَ إِلَى مَا) أَيْ عُضْوٍ (يَدْعُوهُ) أَيْ يَحْمَدُهُ وَيَبْعَثُهُ (إِلَى نِكَاحِهَا فَلْيَفْعَلْ) فَإِنَّهُ مَنْدُوبٌ

[6] al-Marghinani, *al-Hidayah*, 1:185:

(e.g. 'I will marry you') as this indicates uncertainty and possibility.

2. **Witnesses**: i.e. those actually appointed and present at the marriage ceremony or contract:

a) Two Mature (*baligh*), Muslim male witnesses or
b) One mature male and two mature female witnesses;
c) One mature Muslim male and one mature Christian or Jewish male (if a man is marrying someone from the People of the book).[7]

The condition of validity <u>does not</u> include:

3. **Legal marriage guardian (*wali amr*)**: according to the Hanafi School if the woman is a free woman she does not – legally speaking – require a *wali amr* to make her marriage valid but will be sinful for deliberately by-passing him.[8]

"النكاح ينعقد بالإيجاب والقبول بلفظين يعبر بهما عن الماضي" لأن الصيغة وإن كانت للإخبار وضعا فقد جعلت للإنشاء شرعا دفعا للحاجة "وينعقد بلفظين يعبر بأحدهما عن الماضي وبالآخر عن المستقبل مثل أن يقول زوجني فيقول زوجتك

[7] al-Haskafi, *Durr al-Mukhtar* as per Ibn 'Abidin, *Radd al-Muhtar*, 3:21-24:

(وَ) شُرِطَ (حُضُورُ) شَاهِدَيْنِ (حُرَّيْنِ) أَوْ حُرٌّ وَحُرَّتَيْنِ (مُكَلَّفَيْنِ سَامِعَيْنِ قَوْلَهُمَا مَعًا) عَلَى الْأَصَحِّ (فَاهِمَيْنِ) أَنَّهُ نِكَاحٌ عَلَى الْمَذْهَبِ بَحْرٌ (مُسْلِمَيْنِ لِنِكَاحِ مُسْلِمَةٍ وَلَوْ فَاسِقَيْنِ أَوْ مَحْدُودَيْنِ فِي قَذْفٍ أَوْ أَعْمَيَيْنِ أَوْ ابْنَيْ الزَّوْجَيْنِ أَوْ ابْنَيْ أَحَدِهِمَا، وَإِنْ لَمْ يَثْبُتْ النِّكَاحُ بِهِمَا) بِالِابْنَيْنِ (إنْ ادَّعَى الْقَرِيبُ، كَمَا صَحَّ نِكَاحُ مُسْلِمٍ ذِمِّيَّةً عِنْدَ ذِمِّيَّيْنِ)

[8] However, for children, mentally challenged persons and slaves, the legal marriage guardian (*wali amr*) is a condition for the marriage to be valid. In *Durr al-Mukhtar* of al-Haskafi it states, p.183:

<u>Related Rulings</u>:

1. It is not permissible to force a person to marry someone (this is a major sin).
2. It is not permissible to deliberately by-pass the *wali amr* in a marriage procedure (this is a sin).
3. It is not permissible to consider Allah and His Messenger as 'witnesses' to a marriage in place of human beings.
4. It is not permissible to conduct marriage over the phone or internet as witnesses have to actually be present and witness the marriage.[9]
5. It is not permitted to marry without parent's consent (which is a huge act of injustice and sin) although the marriage will be valid.
6. It is permissible to add marital conditions to the marriage contract as long as the conditions do not contradict the Shariah (e.g. the husband cannot act forcefully, he cannot marry a second wife, etc. will not be valid).[10]
7. It is permissible to be engaged but not advisable to unnecessarily delay the marriage.
8. It is permissible for sinful people to be witnesses to a marriage.
9. Marrying a person of the parent's choice is a highly recommended act.

(وَهُوَ) أَيْ الْوَلِيُّ (شَرْطُ) صِحَّةٍ (نِكَاحِ صَغِيرٍ وَمَجْنُونٍ وَرَقِيقٍ) لَا مُكَلَّفَةٍ (فَنَفَذَ نِكَاحُ حُرَّةٍ مُكَلَّفَةٍ بِلَا) رِضَا (وَلِيٍّ)

[9] al-Kasani, *al-Bada'i' al-Sana'i'*, 2:523:

قال عامة العلماء إن الشهادة شرط جواز النكاح

[10] Zafar Usmani, *I'la' al-Sunan*, 11:64 and Ibn 'Abidin, *Radd al-Muhtar*, 2:203.

§4. The Marriage Procedure

The strict legal procedure of marriage is simple in the Shariah and there are no elaborate functions either. The basic sequence of a legal and valid Islamic marriage is as follows:

Step 1: A proposal/offer from A to B where acceptance is expressed in the past tense and in the presence of at least two male Muslim witnesses or one male witness and two female witnesses.[11]

Step 2: The bride is represented by her *mahram* (unmarriageable relative like father, brother, grandfather, etc.). Bride gives her consent to her legal representative (*wakil*) who conducts her marriage before the witnesses with the stipulated dowry agreed beforehand.[12]

Step 3: Marriage is consummated after which it is *sunnah* (recommended act of the Prophet) to hold the wedding feast (*walimah*) and for invitees to attend.[13]

---

[11] al-Marghinani, *al-Hidayah*, 1:185:

قال:النكاح ينعقد بالإيجاب والقبول بلفظين يعبر بهما عن الماضي.

[12] al-Marghinani, *al-Hidayah*, 1:198:

ثم المهر واجب شرعا إبانة لشرف المحل

[13] *al-Fatawa al-Hindiyyah*, 5:343:

وَاخْتُلِفَ فِي إِجَابَةِ الدَّعْوَةِ قَالَ بَعْضُهُمْ وَاجِبَةٌ لَا يَسَعُ تَرْكُهَا وَقَالَتْ الْعَامَّةُ هِيَ سُنَّةٌ وَالْأَفْضَلُ أَنْ يُجِيبَ إذَا كَانت وَلِيمَةً وَإِلَّا فَهُوَ مُخَيَّرٌ وَالْإِجَابَةُ أَفْضَلُ لِأَنَّ فِيهَا إدْخَالَ السُّرُورِ فِي قَلْبِ الْمُؤْمِنِ كَذَا فِي التُّمُرْتَاشِيِّ

Related rulings:

1. It is recommended that the conclusion of the marriage contract/ceremony be carried out in a Mosque.
2. It is permitted to hold a marriage contract ceremony/occasion in one's house.
3. It is permitted for a woman to represent herself in marriage without a legal representative.
4. It is permitted to take a woman's consent (e.g. written down) by representatives and then conveyed to the grooms family (= consent by proxy).
5. It is permitted to refuse any proposal.
6. It is permitted for the bride's party to make an offer of marriage to the groom's party.
7. It is permitted to hold an offer and acceptance feast so long as it is not considered part of the marriage process and Shariah guidelines of gender interaction are followed.
8. It is, strictly speaking, permitted to offer a ring as a gift for the engagement or marriage ceremony as long as it is not considered *necessary* and *part* of the marriage.

§5. The Marriage Event (*Walimah*)

Islam has given broad guidelines on the marriage 'event' or 'feast' (*walimah*)[14] and so there is flexibility for additional details as long as families do not:

---

[14] وَلِيمَة | *walimah*; from the root *w / l / m /* which means 'to gather together' and 'to have something in its completeness'. It refers to more commonly the 'wedding feast'. See Ibn Manzur, *Lisan al-'Arab*, s.v.:

1) Do not contradict text (Qur'an and *hadith*);

2) People do not consider these additions as an intrinsic part of the marriage;

3) Incur burdensome debt and

4) Incur unnecessary excess or wastage (*israf*).

Basic *Walimah* rulings:

1. It is highly recommended (*sunnah mu'akkadah*) to attend a *walimah* invitation (some scholars hold it to be mandatory).[15]
2. It is recommended to invite family, friends, neighbours, pious persons and scholars.[16]
3. It is recommended to offer the *walimah* within two days of the marriage.
4. It is recommended to hold a simple *walimah*.

والوليمةُ طعامُ العُرس والإملاكِ وقيل هي كلُّ طعامٍ صُنع لعُرسٍ ...الوَلْمةُ تمامُ الشيء واجتماعُه وأوْلَمَ الرجلُ إذا اجتمعَ خَلْقُه وعقلُه

[15] Bukhari, *Sahih* (#4872). *al-Fatawa al-Hindiyyah*, 5:343:

وَوَلِيمَةُ الْعُرْسِ سُنَّةٌ وَفِيهَا مَثُوبَةٌ عَظِيمَةٌ

[16] *al-Fatawa al-Hindiyyah*, 5:343:

وَوَلِيمَةُ الْعُرْسِ سُنَّةٌ وَفِيهَا مَثُوبَةٌ عَظِيمَةٌ وَهِيَ إذَا بَنَى الرَّجُلُ بِامْرَأَتِهِ يَنْبَغِي أَنْ يَدْعُوَ الْجِيرَانَ وَالْأَقْرِبَاءَ وَالْأَصْدِقَاءَ وَيَذْبَحَ لهم وَيَصْنَعَ لهم طَعَامًا وإذا اتَّخَذَ يَنْبَغِي لهم أَنْ يُجِيبُوا فَإِنْ لم يَفْعَلُوا أَثِمُوا قال عليه السَّلَامُ من لم يُجِبْ الدَّعْوَةَ فَقَدْ عَصَى اللَّهَ وَرَسُولَهُ

5. It is recommended to talk, converse and speak merrily during the feast to build piety, express joy and happiness (e.g. speak about good matters, relate stories of the pious, etc.).[17]
6. It is permitted to hold a *walimah* in one's house.
7. It is permitted to hold a large and extravagant *walimah* as long as it is within one's means.
8. It is permitted to delay the *walimah* feast to a later date but it will no longer be considered a *walimah*.[18]
9. It is permitted to offer the *walimah* at the time of the marriage contract.
10. It is permitted to offer the *walimah* after the marriage but before consummation.
11. It is permitted to invite people separately for the *walimah*, i.e. on different days due to space, difficulty, etc.
12. It is permitted to decline an offer of attending the *walimah* if one knows the Shariah rulings will be broken (e.g. unlawful music, mixing, etc.).[19]

---

[17] *al-Fatawa al-Hindiyyah*, 5:344:

يُكْرَهُ السُّكُوتُ حَالَةَ الْأَكْلِ لِأَنَّهُ تَشَبُّهٌ بِالْمَجُوسِ كَذَا في السِّرَاجِيَّةِ وَلَا يَسْكُتُ على الطَّعَامِ وَلَكِنْ يَتَكَلَّمُ بِالْمَعْرُوفِ وَحِكَايَاتِ الصَّالِحِينَ كَذَا في الْغَرَائِبِ وَيَنْبَغِي أَنْ يَخْدُمَ الْمُضِيفُ بِنَفْسِهِ اقْتِدَاءً بِإِبْرَاهِيمَ على نَبِيِّنَا وَعَلَيْهِ السَّلَامُ كَذَا في خِزَانَةِ الْمُفْتِينَ

[18] *al-Fatawa al-Hindiyyah*, 5:343-344:

وَلَا بَأْسَ بِأَنْ يَدْعُوَ يَوْمَئِذٍ مِن الْغَدِ وَبَعْدَ الْغَدِ ثُمَّ يَنْقَطِعُ الْعُرْسُ وَالْوَلِيمَةُ كَذَا في الظَّهِيرِيَّةِ

[19] *al-Fatawa al-Hindiyyah*, 5:343:

من دُعِيَ إلَى وَلِيمَةٍ فَوَجَدَ ثَمَّةَ لَعِبًا أو غِنَاءً فَلَا بَأْسَ أَنْ يَقْعُدَ وَيَأْكُلَ فَإِنْ قَدَرَ على الْمَنْعِ يَمْنَعُهُمْ وَإِنْ لم يَقْدِرْ يَصْبِرُ وَهَذَا إذَا لم يُكُنْ مُقْتَدًى بِهِ أَمَّا إذَا كان ولم يَقْدِرْ على مَنْعِهِمْ فإنه يَخْرُجُ وَلَا يَقْعُدُ وَلَوْ كان ذلك على الْمَائِدَةِ لَا يَنْبَغِي أَنْ يَقْعُدَ وَإِنْ لم يُكُنْ مُقْتَدًى بِهِ وَهَذَا كُلُّهُ بَعْدَ الْحُضُورِ وَأَمَّا إذَا عَلِمَ قبل الْحُضُورِ فَلَا يَحْضُرُ

13. It is permitted to use food agencies or caterers to organise the *walimah* event under the laws of agency (*wakalah*).

Some related rulings of the marriage 'event' include the following:

1. It is permissible to offer and exchange gifts as part of the process before the actual marriage.
2. It is permissible to invite families for pre-wedding feasts for bonding as long as there are no impermissible elements (e.g. unlawful mixing, etc.).
3. It is permissible to sing permissible songs of joy as long as no Shariah rulings on music and interaction are broken.
4. It is not permissible to follow established customs of other religions.
5. It is not permissible to unlawfully mix wedding guests.

§6. Marriageable and Unmarriageable Persons

There are three relationships that must be considered in order to know who a person can marry and who they cannot:

1] those by **lineage**/blood (*nasab*);

2] those by **fosterage**/suckling (*rada'ah*) and

لِأَنَّهُ لَا يَلْزَمُهُ حَقُّ الدَّعْوَةِ بِخِلَافِ ما إذا هَجَمَ عليه لِأَنَّهُ قد لَزِمَهُ كَذَا في السِّرَاج الوَهَّاج وَإِنْ عَلِمَ الْمُقْتَدَى بِهِ بِذَلِكَ قبل الدُّخُول وهو مُحْتَرَمٌ يَعْلَمُ أَنَّهُ لو دخل يَتْرُكُونَ ذلك فَعَلَيْهِ أَنْ يَدْخُلَ وَإِلَّا لم يَدْخُلْ كَذَا في التُّمُرْتَاشِيِّ

3] those by **marriage** (*sihriyyah/musaharah*).[20]

A *mahram* (literally = 'a person who is unlawful') is anyone who becomes permanently forbidden to marry whether through blood relations, fostering or marriage.[21] The term *ghayr mahram* refers to those who one is permitted to marry by Law. Below is a table outlining **unmarriageable** persons according to these three types of relationships:

LINEAGE	FOSTERAGE[22]	MARRIAGE
1. Mother.	1. Foster mother.	In the case of a man:
2. Grandmother.	2. Foster father.	1. Mother-in-law
3. Great-grandmother, etc.	3. Foster brother.	2. Mother-in-law's mother (wife's grandmother).
4. Father.	4. Foster sister.	3. Wife's daughter from a previous marriage.
5. Grandfather.	5. Foster uncle.	
6. Great-grandfather etc.	6. Foster Aunt.	
7. Sons.	7. Foster nephew.	4. Wife's granddaughter.
8. Grandsons.	8. Foster niece.	5. Wife's son's daughter.
9. Great-grandsons, etc.	9. Etc.	6. Wife's daughter's daughter.
10. Daughters.		7. The wife of
11. Grand-daughters.		
12. Great-granddaughters, etc.		
13. All types of sisters (half and full).		

---

[20] al-Kasani, *al-Bada'i' al-Sana'i'*, 2:124:

صفة المحرم أن يكون ممن لا يجوز له نكاحها على التأبيد إما بالقرابة ، أو الرضاع، أو الصهرية؛ لأن الحرمة المؤبدة تزيل التهمة في الخلوة

[21] al-Marghinani, *al-Hidayah*, 4:461-462.
[22] Whoever is a *mahram* through the relationship of lineage, will also be considered a *mahram* by fosterage.

14. Maternal aunts (mother's sister).	**Foster relationships are treated identically as blood relationships**.	one's son, grandson, and on down.
15. Paternal aunts (father's sister).		8. Step-mother.
16. Nieces (brother's daughter and sister's daughter).		9. Step-grandmother.

In the case of a woman:

10. Father-in-law.
11. Father-in-law's father (husband's grandmother).
12. Husband's son from a previous marriage.
13. Husband's grandson.
14. Husband's daughter's son.
15. The husband of one's daughter, granddaughter and on down.
16. Step-father.
17. Step-grandfather.

§7. Forbidden Relations and Incest

In the Shariah, there are rulings which address certain delicate scenarios that have an implication on a person's marriage and lawful relationships. These are cases of incest or *hurmat al-musaharah* ('that which permanently forbids a person from marrying another person' or 'marriage being forbidden because of touching').[23] For the Hanafi

---

[23] See for example:

Fatawa Qadi Khan, 11:177:

jurists, if two matters occur with regard to a person, then both ascendants and descendants of each person involved

---

وإن مسها وعليها ثوب صفيق لا تصل حرارة الممسوسة ولينها إلى يده لا تثبت الحرمة...

ودليل الشهوة على قول أبي الحسن القمي رحمه الله تعالى انتشار الآلة عند ذلك إن لم يكن منتشراً قبل ذلك وإن كان منتشراً قبل ذلك فعلامة الشهوة زيادة الانتشار والشدة

al-Fatawa al-Hindiyyah, 1:275:

ثم المس إنما يوجب حرمة المصاهرة إذا لم يكن بينهما ثوب، أما إذا كان بينهما ثوب فإن كان صفيقا لا يجد الماس حرارة الممسوس لا تثبت حرمة المصاهرة وإن انتشرت آلته بذلك...

Ibn 'Abidin, *Radd al-Muhtar*, 4:112:

وظاهره اعتبار السن الآتي في حد المشتهاة أعني تسع سنين...فتحصل من هذا : أنه لا بد في كل منهما من سن المراهقة وأقله للأنثى تسع...

al-Bukhari, *al-Muhit al-Burhani*, 3:63-64:

قال الفقيه أبو الليث رحمه الله في «أيمان الفتاوى» : المشايخ سكتوا في الثمان والتسع والغالب أنها لا تشتهي ما لم تبلغ تسع سنين قال الصدر الشهيد رحمه الله في شرح كتاب النفقات وعليه الفتوى، وحكي عن الشيخ الإمام أبي بكر هذا رحمه الله أنه كان يقول: ينبغي للمفتي أن يفتي في السبع، والثمان أنها لا تحرم إلا إذا بالغ السائل أنها عبلة ضخمة وجسيمة فحينئذ يفتي بالحرمة...

وحد الشهوة في الرجل أن تنتشر آلته أو تزداد انتشارا إن كانت منتشرة، كذا في التبيين. وهو الصحيح، كذا في جواهر الأخلاطي. وبه يفتى كذا في الخلاصة. فمن انتشرت آلته فطلب امرأته وأولجها بين فخذي ابنتها لا تحرم عليه أمها ما لم تزدد انتشارا، كذا في التبيين...

والشهوة: أن تنتشر آلته إليه بالنظر إلى الفرج أو المس إذا لم يكن منتشرا قبل هذا، وإذا كان منتشرا فإن كان يزداد قوة بالنظر والمس كان ذلك عن شهوة وما (لا) فلا... وروى ابن رستم عن محمد رحمه الله: أنه إذا لمسها بشهوة فلم ينتشر عضوه أو كان منتشرا فلم يزدد انتشاره حتى تركها ثم ازداد انتشاره بعد لم تثبت به الحرمة، وإنما تثبت الحرمة إذا انتشر بالمس وهو بعد لامسها، أو يزداد انتشاره وهو لامسها

will be forbidden with each other. The two matters are the following:

[1] Touching a person unlawful to marry without any thick barrier on the skin such that the heat of the skin can be felt intentionally or unintentionally out of lust and sexual desire;[24]

[2] Having sex with a person one is *mahram* with by marriage.

Some related rulings include:

1. If a married man commits an incestuous act (touching or other) with his daughter, his wife becomes permanently forbidden to him and the children become illegitimate (i.e. paternity cannot be attributed to him).
2. Mere touching does not fall under an incestuous act or *hurmat al-musaharah*.
3. Any incestuous inclination that is subsequent to a touch does not establish *hurmat al-musaharah*.

---

[24] شهوة | By *shahawah* ('desire', 'lust', 'passion') with respect to: i) a man, it means an erection or increase in erection if it already exists and ii) with respect to elderly persons and women, it is defined as an intense and burning desire that clouds one's judgment. These emotions must exist at the point of contact. If it happens afterwards, there is no legal consequence. 'Ala' al-Din, *al-Hadiyyah al-'Ala'iyyah*, p.352. See also Ibn al-Humam, *Fath al-Qadir*, 3:129:

ما الشيخ والعنين فحدها تحرك قلبه أو زيادة تحركه إن كان متحركا لا مجرد ميلان النفس فإنه يوجد فيمن لا شهوة له أصلا كالشيخ الفاني، والمراهق كالبالغ، حتى لو مس وأقر أنه بشهوة تثبت الحرمة عليه

The Prophet said:

تُنكَحُ المرأةُ لأربعٍ : لِمَالِهَا ، وَلِحَسَبِهَا، وَجَمَالِهَا ، وَلِدِينِهَا، فَاظفَر بِذَاتِ الدِّينِ تَرِبَت يَدَاكَ

"Women may be married for four things: their wealth, their lineage, their beauty and their religious commitment. Choose the one who is religiously-committed, may your hands be rubbed with dust (i.e., may you prosper)." (Bukhari, *Sahih* [#4802])

Chapter 2: Dowry, Suitability and Expenses: *Some Marriage Elements to Understand"*

Below are outlines of some key elements of a marriage that require correct knowledge. They are mentioned with their related rulings with contemporary applications and practices.

——————— Γ ———————

§1. *Mahr* (Dowry)

المهر I *mahr*; dower, dowry, money given as a wedding gift; any assets a woman acquires through marriage.[25]

- Two matters necessitate the payment of the woman's dowry:

[1] **Sexual intercourse**: i.e. minimal act being penetration.

[2] **Being in seclusion (*khalwah sahihah*)**: which is defined as being in a place where two persons are alone without fear of a third intruding or knowing and no physical prevention from both having sex.[26]

_____

[25] al-Haskafi, *Durr al-Mukhtar*, 3:101:

ومن أسمائه : الصداق والصدقة، والنحلة، والعطية، والعقر

[26] al-Mawsili, *al-Ikhtiyar li-Ta'lil al-Mukhtar*, 3:137-138:

والخلوة الصحيحة أن لا يكون ثم مانع من الوطء طبعا وشرعا، فالمرض المانع من الوطء من جهته أو جهتها مانع طبعا، وكذلك الرتق والقرن)، وكذا إذا كان يخاف زيادة المرض، فإنه لا يعرى عن نوع فتور، (والحيض (مانع شرعا وطبعا إذ الطباع السليمة تنفر منه، (والإحرام) بالحج أو العمرة فرضا أو نفلا، (وصوم

- Dowry is mandatory to give by the groom to the bride.[27]
- A dowry is the right of a woman and a measure of the husband's honour for her and gratitude to Allah.
- A marriage is still legally valid even if the dowry was not stipulated or mentioned at the time of the marriage contract.
- If no dowry was stipulated at all, then a 'typical' or 'similar' dowry will be given (*mahr mithl*), i.e. a dowry that similar brides received from the wife's father's side (e.g. her sisters, paternal aunties and their daughters, etc).[28] The way 'similar' is

---

رمضان وصلاة الفرض) مانع شرعا ...والمكان الذي تصح فيه الخلوة أن يأمنا فيه اطلاع غيرهما عليهما حتى لو خلا بها في مسجد أو حمام أو طريق أو على سطح لا حجاب له فليست صحيحة، وكذلك لو كان معهما أعمى أو صبي يعقل أو مجنون أو كلب عقور أو منكوحة له أخرى أو أجنبية، وفي الأمة فيه روايتان، وعليها العدة في جميع ذلك احتياطا؛ لأنها حق الشرع .

[27] Ibn Nujaym, *Bahr al-Ra'iq*, 3:152:

(قوله صح النكاح بلا ذكره) لأن النكاح عقد انضمام وازدواج لغة فيتم بالزوجين ثم المهر واجب شرعا إبانة لشرف المحل فلا يحتاج إلى ذكره لصحة النكاح

[28] al-Mawsili, *al-Ikhtiyar li-Ta'lil al-Mukhtar*, 3:136:

قال : (وإن لم يسم لها مهرا أو شرط أن لا مهر لها فلها مهر المثل بالدخول والموت والمتعة بالطلاق قبل الدخول) لأن النكاح صح فيجب العوض لأنه عقد معاوضة، والمهر وجب حقا للشرع على ما بينا، والواجب الأصلي مهر المثل لأنه أعدل فيصار إليه عند عدم التسمية، بخلاف حالة التسمية لأنهم رضوا به، فإن كان أقل من مهر المثل فقد رضيت بالنقصان، وإن كان أكثر فقد رضي بالزيادة . قال – عليه الصلاة والسلام : – "المهر ما تراضى عليه الأهلو " ، وقد صح أن النبي – صلى الله عليه وسلم – قضى في بروع بنت واشق الأشجعية بمهر المثل، وقد تزوجت بغير مهر ومات عنها قبل الدخول . وأما وجوب المتعة بالطلاق قبل الدخول فلقوله – تعالى – فيه : (ومتعوهن على الموسع قدره وعلى المقتر قدره)

determined is consideration of age, beauty, virginity, place, time and economic standing. Comparison will be made and the wife will be given the dowry measured according to one of them.[29]

- The minimum amount of dowry is 10 dirham (= 31g of silver).[30] Some say it is 500 dirhams (= 1530g of silver) and others say 400 *mithqal* (= 1750g silver).[31]

- There is in principle, no maximum limit for a dowry.

- Excessive amounts of dowry should not be stipulated.[32]

- It is allowed to give dowry in non-cash form, e.g. jewellery or gifts.

- It is allowed for the woman to ask for the immediate amount of the total dowry.

- It is allowed for the woman to waive her dowry.

- It is allowed for the woman to reduce/decrease her dowry.

---

[29] al-Mawsili, *al-Ikhtiyar li-Ta'lil al-Mukhtar*, 3:144:

قال (: ومهر مثلها يعتبر بنساء عشيرة أبيها) كأخواتها وعماتها وبنات عمها دون أمها وخالتها إلا أن يكونا من قبيلة أبيها، هكذا روي عن رسول الله – صلى الله عليه وسلم – في بروع حين تزوجت بغير مهر، فقال : " لها مهر مثل نسائها " ونساؤها أقارب الأب، ولأن قيمة الشيء تعرف بقيمة جنسه، وجنسه قوم أبيه . (فإن لم يوجد منهم مثل حالها فمن الأجانب) تحصيلا للمقصود بقدر الوسع . قال : (ويعتبر بامرأة هي مثلها في السن والحسن والبكارة والبلد والعصر والمال) فإن المهر يختلف باختلاف هذه الأوصاف لأن الرغبات تختلف بها . فإن لم يوجد ذلك كله فالذي يوجد منه) لأنه يتعذر اجتماع هذه الأوصاف في امرأتين فيعتبر بالموجود منها لأنها مثلها . وعن بعض المشايخ أن الجمال لا يعتبر إذا كانت ذات حسب وشرف، وإنما يعتبر في الأوسط لأن الرغبة حينئذ في الجمال

[30] Ibn Nujaym, *Bahr al-Ra'iq*, 3:152:

قوله (وأقله عشرة دراهم) أي أقل المهر شرعا للحديث 'لا مهر أقل من عشرة دراهم' وهو وإن كان ضعيفا

[31] 'Ali al-Qari, *Mirqat al-Mafatih*, 6:246.
[32] Tirmidhi, *Sunan* (#1114).

- It is allowed for the dowry to be given in instalments by the husband.
- It is allowed for the husband to pay dowry more than the minimum amount but if he consummates the marriage he is bound to it.
- It is allowed for a portion of the dowry to be deferred to a later date, e.g. the husband's death or divorce where upon maturity of that date or event, the woman will receive the rest of her dowry.[33]
- It is allowed to negotiate a dowry quantity.
- It is not allowed to ask the groom's side for more than the obligatory dowry amount (e.g. extra gifts, additional goods, etc.) as this is tantamount to bribery (*rishwah*) in the Shariah.[34]
- If a husband was secluded with his wife without any barriers to them having sex but he divorces his wife, she is entitled to a full dowry.[35]

---

[33] Ibn 'Abidin, *Radd al-Muhtar*, 3:144:

قلت : والمتعارف في زماننا في مصر والشام تعجيل الثلثين وتأجيل الثلث

[34] Ibn 'Abidin, *Radd al-Muhtar*, 3:155-156:

(قوله عند التسليم) أي بأن لا يسلمها أخوها أو نحوه حتى يأخذ شيئا، وكذا لو أبى أن يزوجها فللزوج الاسترداد قائما أو هالكا لأنه رشوة بزازية . وفي الحاوي الزاهدي برمز الأسرار للعلامة نجم الدين : وإن أعطى إلى رجل شيئا لإصلاح مصالح المصاهرة إن كان من قوم الخطيبة أو غيرهم الذين يقدرون على الإصلاح والفساد وقال هو أجرة لك على الإصلاح لا يرجع وإن قال على عدم الفساد والسكوت يرجع لأنه رشوة، والأجرة إنما تكون في مقابلة العمل والسكوت ليس بعمل وإن لم يقل هو أجرة يرجع وإن كان ممن يقدرون على ذلك، إن قال هو عطية أو أجرة لك على الذهاب والإياب أو الكلام أو الرسالة بيني وبينها لا يرجع، وإن لم يقل شيئا منها يكون هبة له الرجوع فيها إن لم يوجد ما يمنع الرجوع

[35] Ibn al-Humam, *Fath al-Qadir*, 3:332:

- If the husband divorced his wife prior to any sexual intercourse or intimate contact, then she is entitled to **half** the <u>stipulated</u> dowry.[36]

(وإذا خلا الرجل بامرأته وليس هناك مانع من الوطء ثم طلقها فلها كمال المهر) وقال الشافعي : لها نصف المهر لأن المعقود عليه إنما يصير مستوفى بالوطء فلا يتأكد المهر دونه ولنا أنها سلمت المبدل حيث رفعت الموانع وذلك وسعها فيتأكد حقها في البدل اعتبارا بالبيع

[36] Ibid., 3:328-329:

(وإن تزوجها ولم يسم لها مهرا ثم تراضيا على تسمية فهي لها إن دخل بها أو مات عنها، وإن طلقها قبل الدخول بها فلها المتعة) وعلى قول أبي يوسف الأول نصف هذا المفروض وهو قول الشافعي لأنه مفروض فيتنصف بالنص . ولنا أن هذا الفرض تعيين للواجب بالعقد وهو مهر المثل وذلك لا يتنصف : فكذا ما نزل منزلته، والمراد بما تلا الفرض في العقد إذ هو الفرض المتعارف . .

(قوله وعلى قول أبي يوسف الأول) إشارة إلى أن قوله الآخر كقولهما (قوله فيتنصف بالنص) يعني قوله تعالى { فنصف ما فرضتم } فإنه يتناول ما فرض في العقد أو بعده بتراضيهما أو بفرض القاضي فإن لها أن ترفعه إلى القاضي ليفرض لها إذا لم يكن فرض لها في العقد (قوله إن هذا الفرض تعيين لمهر المثل) وذلك ؛ لأن هذا العقد حين انعقد كان موجبا لمهر المثل؛ لأن ذلك حكم العقد الذي لم يسم فيه مهر، وثبوت الملزوم لا يتخلف عنه ثبوت اللازم، فإذا كان الثابت به لزوم مهر المثل لا يتنصف إجماعا فلا يتنصف ما فرض بعد العقد . والفرض المنصف في النص : أعني قوله تعالى { فنصف ما فرضتم } يجب حينئذ حمله على المفروض في العقد بالضرورة؛ لأنا لما بينا أن المفروض بعد عقد لا تسمية فيه هو نفس خصوص مهر مثل تلك المرأة، وأن الإجماع على عدم انتصافه لزم بالضرورة أن المتنصف بالنص ما فرض في العقد، على أن : المتعارف هو الفرض في العقد حتى كان المتبادر من قولنا فرض لها الصداق أنه أوجبه في العقد فيقيد لذلك نص فرضتم به ضرورة أن المخبر عنه بفرضتم هو الفرض الواقع في العقد، وهذا من المصنف تقييد بالعرف العملي بعدما منع منه في الفصل السابق حيث قال : أو هو عرف عملي، ولا يصلح مقيدا للفظ، وقدمنا أن الحق التقييد به . وفي الغاية والدراية : لا يتناول غيره : أي غير المفروض في العقد إذ المطلق لا عموم له وليس بشيء، لأن المطلق هو المتعرض لمجرد الذات فيتناول المفروض على أي صفة كانت سواء كان في العقد أو بعده بتراضيهما أو بفرض القاضي عليه لو رافعته ليفرض لها . فالصواب ما ذكرنا من أن المفروض بعد العقد نفس مهر المثل، وأن الفرض لتعيين كميته ليمكن دفعه، وهو لا يتنصف إجماعا فتعين كون المراد به في النص المتعارف دون غيره مما يصدق عليه لغة لما بينا، ولأن غيره غير متبادر لندرة وجوده

- If the husband divorced his wife prior to any sexual intercourse or intimate contact, and no exact dowry figure was stipulated, then she is entitled to an amenity payment (*mut'ah*) or gift.[37]

- If the husband divorced his wife having sexual intercourse or intimate contact with her and no exact dowry figure was stipulated, then she is entitled to a typical dowry (*mahr mithl*).

- If a judge (*qadi*) decrees a separation between a man and a woman prior to their consummation of the marriage, the woman would not be entitled to dowry because the acquisition of benefits was not realised, viz. physical contact. Merely signing a marriage contract does not obligate the husband for dowry.

- If the husband is impotent or has reduced sexual mobility but was in seclusion with his wife, she is entitled to the full dowry because she has completed her part of the marital obligation (i.e. *taslim* [submission/making herself present for the husband]).[38]

---

[37] al-Haskafi, *Durr al-Mukhtar*, 3:110:

(و) تجب (متعة لمفوضة) وهي من زوجت بلا مهر (طلقت قبل الوطء، وهي درع وخمار وملحفة لا تزيد على نصفه) أي نصف مهر المثل لو الزوج غنيا (ولا تنقص عن خمسة دراهم (لو فقيرا) :وتعتبر) المتعة (بحالهما) كالنفقة به يفتى

[38] Ibn al-Humam, *Fath al-Qadir*, 3:334:

وإذا خلا المجبوب بامرأته ثم طلقها فلها كمال المهر عند أبي حنيفة، وقالا عليه نصف المهر) لأنه أعجز من المريض ، بخلاف العنين لأن الحكم أدير على سلامة الآلة . ولأبي حنيفة أن المستحق عليها التسليم في حق السحق وقد أتت به .

§2. *Kafa'ah* (Suitability)

الكفؤ | *kufu'*; also written as *kafa'ah*; suitability, compatibility and affinity – especially in marriage.

- *Kafa'ah* is considered from the perspective of the <u>woman only</u> and not the man, i.e. the suitability of a man for a woman is considered and not vice versa. This is because the texts have come specifying this to her only.[39]

- **The aim of *kafa'ah***: It is allowed for a woman to emphasise suitability as a marital consideration for harmony of her marriage, overall stability of the family and contentment – which are some of the key aims of marriage.

- *Kafa'ah* is considered from the following aspects:[40]

[1] **Lineage**: this is only amongst Arabs (defined as being a family being traced back to an Arab tribe) because they pride themselves in their lineage and based on the Prophet's narrations that **"Quraysh are suitable for each other and all Arabs are suitable for each other"**;

---

[39] al-Kasani, *al-Bada'i' al-Sana'i'*, 3:319:

الكفاءة تعتبر للنساء لا للرجال على معنى أنه تعتبر الكفاءة في جانب الرجال للنساء و لا تعتبر في جانب النساء للرجال لأن النصوص وردت بالاعتبار في جانب الرجال خاصة

[40] al-Mawsili, *al-Ikhtiyar li-Ta'lil al-Mukhtar*, 3:132:

والكفاءة تعتبر في النكاح في النسب وفي الدين والتقوى وفي الصنائع وفي الحرّية وفي المال

[2] **Islam**: Muslim ancestry is considered in non-Arabs and not Arabs and is considered from the father and grandfather's side (patrilineal ascription);[41]

[3] **Piety**: i.e. the degree of religiosity of a woman and compatibility in religiosity;

[4] **Profession**: this is considered mainly in non-Arabs and refers to compatibility in professional levels, usually determined by assessing the suitor's job being similar to the wife's father's job. The social standing of each profession is determined by the local customs of both partners;[42] – Abu Hanifah did not consider this as an intrinsic aspect related to suitability as he believed there could be social mobility amongst people and so a person can attain a higher social standing through their efforts.[43]

---

[41] al-Marghinani, *al-Hidayah*, 1:96:

وأما الموالي فمن كان له أبوان في الإسلام فصاعدا فهو من الأكفاء يعني لمن له آباء فيه ومن أسلم بنفسه أو له أب واحد في الإسلام لا يكون كفؤا لمن له أبوان في الإسلام لأن تمام النسب بالأب والجد

[42] al-Kasani, *al-Bada'i' al-Sana'i'*, 2:320:

ذكر القاضي في شرحه مختصر الطحاوي اعتبار الكفاءة في الحرفة ولم يذكر الخلاف فتثبت الكفاءة بين الحرفتين في جنس واحد كالبزاز مع البزاز والحائك مع الحائك وتثبت عند اختلاف جنس الحرف إذا كان يقارب بعضها بعضا كالبزاز مع الصائغ والصائغ مع العطار والحائك مع الحجام والحجام مع الدباغ ولا تثبت فيما لا مقاربة بينهما كالعطار مع البيطار والبزاز مع الخراز

[43] al-Mawsili, *al-Ikhtiyar li-Ta'lil al-Mukhtar*, 3:133:

قال) : وفي الصنائع (لأن الناس يعيرون بالدنيء منها . وعن أبي حنيفة أنه غير معتبر فإنه يمكن الانتقال عنها فليست وصفا لازما . وعن أبي يوسف لا يعتبر إلا أن يفحش كالحائك والحجام والكناس والدباغ فإنه لا يكون كفؤا لبنت البزاز والعطار والصيرفي والجوهري

[5] **Freedom**: a free woman is not suitable for a male slave and

[6] **Wealth**: this entails either (a) possessing the dowry amount that is customarily paid up front (*mahr mithl*); (b) being able to provide for the wife daily if employed or (c) possessing a monthly provision for one's wife if unemployed.[44]

- It is not suitable for non-Arabs to marry Arabs from the tribe of Quraysh.
- It is not suitable for a Muslim man who has a non-Muslim father to marry a Muslim woman who does have a Muslim father.
- It is not suitable for a Muslim man who has a Muslim father but non-Muslim grandfather to marry a woman whose paternal grandfather is a Muslim.
- It is not suitable for non-religious man to marry a religious woman with a religious father.
- It is not suitable for a man with a comparatively lower social profession to marry a woman in a higher social profession.
- It is not allowed to prevent a marriage that has full compatibility between spouses.
- It is not allowed to base compatibility on astrological considerations (e.g. as in Hindu practices).

---

[44] al-Kasani, *al-Bada'i' al-Sana'i'*, 2:321:

المعتبر فيه القدرة على مهر مثلها والنفقة ولا تعتبر الزيادة على ذلك... وإن كان لا يساويها في المال، هكذا روي عن أبي حنيفة وأبي يوسف ومحمد في ظاهر الروايات

- If the legal guardian of the marriage objects to a marriage on the grounds of suitability (*kafa'ah*), then the objection is valid.
- If the legal guardian objects to a marriage based on unsuitability, then the marriage itself will be invalid according to the *fatwa position* of the Hanafi School.
- If the legal guardian objects to a marriage based on unsuitability, then the marriage will still be valid according to the *established position* from Imam Abu Hanifah but the legal guardian would be entitled to take the matter to the Islamic courts for dissolution of the marriage.
- If the legal guardian and the wife agree to a partner for marriage that is unsuitable then the marriage is valid – even if later they regret it.
- *Kafa'ah* is only given consideration at the **beginning** of the marriage process such that if a woman married a person of high standing and later that person of high standing loses his post or position, this cannot be a grounds to annul the marriage contract as it is impossible for a person to maintain his exact circumstances throughout his life and so it cannot be stipulated as a condition for a marriage contract.[45]
- *Kafa'ah* generally does not hold when it comes to inter-*madhhab* marriages.[46]

---

[45] Qudri Paşa, *al-Ahwal al-Shakhsiyyah*, art.62:

والكفاءة حق الولي وحق المرآة واعتبارها عند ابتداء العقد فلا يضر زوالها بعده

[46] Ibn 'Abidin, *Radd al-Muhtar*, 3:93.

Kafa'ah – a rejoinder

- In 'Abd al-Wahhab Khallaf's *al-Ahwal al-Shakhsiyyah fi Shari'at al-Islamiyyah*, p.73 it concludes:

  "Some of the scholars do not consider *kafa'ah* as valid whatsoever because all people are equal. The Prophet (saw) has said: **'People are equal like the teeth of a comb; an Arab is not superior to a non-Arab. Superiority is established only on the basis of piety (*taqwa*)'.** He also said: **'O tribe of Hashim! People will not come to me with [good] deeds but with their lineage. Indeed, the most honourable of you in the sight of Allah is he who is most conscious and fearing of Allah'.** Any [Muslim] man is therefore suitable for a woman whatever her origin…"

وبعض الأئمة لا يعتبر الكفاءة مطلقاً لأن الناس سواء وقد قال ﷺ : « الناس سواسية كأسنان المشط لا فضل لعربى على عجمى إنما الفضل بالتقوى » وقال : « يا بنى هاشم لا يجيئنى الناس بالأعمال وتجيئونى بالأنساب إن أكرمكم عند الله أتقاكم » فكل مسلم كفء لأية امرأة مهما كان أصلها .

- This perhaps is the soundest position. And Allah knows best.[47]

---

[47] For a detailed discussion on this, see al-Nabhani, *Nizam al-Ijtima'i fi'l-Islam*, pp.104-108.

§3. *Nafaqah* (Maintenance)

النفقة | *nafaqah*; maintenance, financial support; expenses and family costs.

- *Nafaqah* is of different types:

(1) those for one's spouse;
(2) those for one's relatives;
(3) those for one's slaves and
(4) those for one's animals/pets.[48]

- The entitlements under *nafaqah* include the following:[49]

---

[48] al-Kasani, *al-Bada'i' al-Sana'i'*, 4:15:

النفقة أنواع أربعة : نفقة الزوجات، ونفقة الأقارب، ونفقة الرقيق، ونفقة البهائم والجمادات

[49] See *al-Fatawa al-Hinidyyah*, 1:549:

وَالنَّفَقَةُ الْوَاجِبَةُ الْمَأْكُولُ وَالْمَلْبُوسُ وَالسُّكْنَى أَمَّا الْمَأْكُولُ فَالدَّقِيقُ وَالْمَاءُ وَالْمِلْحُ وَالْحَطَبُ وَالدُّهْنُ كَذَا فِي التَّتَارْخَانِيَّةِ وَكَمَا يُفْرَضُ لها قَدْرُ الْكِفَايَةِ من الطَّعَامِ كَذَلِكَ من الْآدَامِ كَذَا فِي فَتْحِ الْقَدِيرِ وَيَجِبُ لها ما تُنَظَّفُ بِهِ وَتُزِيلُ الْوَسَخَ كَالْمُشْطِ وَالدُّهْنِ وما تَغْسِلُ بِهِ من السِّدْرِ وَالْخِطْمِيُّ وما تُزِيلُ بِهِ الدَّرَنَ كَالْأُشْنَانِ وَالصَّابُون على عَادَةِ أَهْلِ الْبَلَدِ وَأَمَّا ما يُقْصَدُ بِهِ التَّلَذُّذُ وَالِاسْتِمْتَاعُ مِثْلُ الْخِضَابِ وَالْكُحْلِ فَلَا يَلْزَمُهُ بَلْ هو على اخْتِيَارِهِ إنْ شَاءَ هَيَّأَهُ لها وَإِنْ شَاءَ تَرَكَهُ فإذا هَيَّأَهُ لها فَعَلَيْهَا اسْتِعْمَالُهُ وَأَمَّا الطِّيبُ فَلَا يَجِبُ عليه منه إلَّا ما يَقْطَعُ بِهِ السَّهُوكَةَ لَا غَيْرُ وَيَجِبُ عليه ما يَقْطَعُ بِهِ الصُّنَانَ وَلَا يَجِبُ الدَّوَاءُ لِلْمَرَضِ وَلَا أُجْرَةُ الطَّبِيبِ وَلَا الْفَصْدُ وَلَا الْحِجَامَةُ كَذَا فِي السِّرَاجِ الْوَهَّاجِ وَعَلَيْهِ من الْمَاءِ ما تَغْسِلُ بِهِ ثِيَابَهَا وَبَدَنَهَا من الْوَسَخِ كَذَا فِي الْجَوْهَرَةِ النَّيِّرَةِ وفي فَتَاوَى أبي اللَّيْثِ رَحِمَهُ اللَّهُ تَعَالَى ثَمَنُ مَاءِ الِاغْتِسَالِ على الزَّوْجِ وَكَذَا مَاءُ وُضُوئِهَا عليه غَنِيَّةً كَانت أو فَقِيرَةً وفي الصَّيْرَفِيَّةِ وَعَلَيْهِ فَتْوَى مَشَايِخِ بَلْخٍ وَفَتْوَى الصَّدْرِ الشَّهِيدِ رَحِمَهُ اللَّهُ تَعَالَى وهو اخْتِيَارُ قَاضِي خَانْ كَذَا فِي التَّتَارْخَانِيَّةِ ...

(1) **Food**: essentials such as oil, flour, salt, meat, vegetables, etc which includes utensils.

(2) **Clothing**: for different seasons and climates which excludes luxuries (as these are optional on the husband to pay for).

(3) **Shelter**: a private room, apartment, house or a separate enclosed space – depending on circumstances and need which must be safe and secure from intrusion.

(4) **Other necessities**: i.e. items of necessity both for her and her domestic duties, e.g. cleaning products which includes utility bills as they are both part of the house and necessary, etc.

- *Nafaqah* is mandatory on the husband.[50]
- *Nafaqah* is determined by the status and circumstances of both the husband and the wife: if both are wealthy, then the *nafaqah* must be given accordingly and if they are not wealthy, then again the *nafaqah* has to be accordingly. There is no quantification (i.e. a financial figure) of the *nafaqah* only what is sufficient to the circumstances based on the customs of that locality/region.[51]

---

[50] Qudri Paşa, *al-Ahkam al-Shar'iyyah fi 'l-Ahwal al-Shakhsiyyah*, art.160:

تجب النفقة من حين العقد الصحيح على الزوج ولو فقيراً أو مريضاً أو عنيناً أو صغيراً لا يقدر على المباشرة للزوجة غنية كانت أو فقيرة مسلمة أو غير مسلمة كبيرة أو صغيرة تطيق الوقاع أو تشتهي له

[51] Ibid., art:173:

- *Nafaqah* is mandatory because of either:

(1) marriage itself,

(2) because men have been put in charge of women (*qawwamun*)

(3) because she is constrained to him in his house through marriage and hence he must look-after what is in his possession (the latter view is the general Hanafi position).

- *Nafaqah* can be given daily, weekly or monthly based on the husband's job and circumstances or even based on a prior and agreed arrangement with the wife.[52]
- *Nafaqah* can be given in advance as well, e.g. a month, 2 months 6 months or even a year's expenses and should there be a divorce in between, the *nafaqah* does not have to be returned.[53]

تقدر نفقة الطعام بقدر حال الزوجين يساراً وإعساراً فإن كانا موسرين فنفقة اليسار وإن كانا معسرين فنفقة الإعسار وإن كانا مختلفين حالاً فنفقة الوسط فلو كان الزوج هو الفقير لا يخاطب إلا بقدر وسعه والباقي دين عليه إلى الميسرة

[52] Ibid., art:175:

يعتبر في فرض النفقة وإعطائها للمرآة الأصلح والأيسر فإن كان الزوج محترفاً يكتسب قوته كل يوم تقدر النفقة عليه يوماً بيوم ويعطيها نفقة كل يوم معجلاً عند مساء اليوم الذي قبله

وإن كان من الصناع الذين لا ينقضي عملهم إلا بمضي أسبوع تقدر عليه كل أسبوع

وإن كان تاجراً أو من أرباب الماهيات تفرض عليه كل شهر وإن كان مزارعاً تفرض عليه كل سنة فإن ماطلها الزوج في دفع النفقة في مواعيدها المقررة فلها أن تطلب نفقة كل يوم

[53] Ibid., art:203:

- A wife is entitled to *nafaqah* even if she is living in her father's house, e.g. on holiday, visitation, etc.[54]
- A wife is entitled to *nafaqah* even if she refuses to travel with her husband or is unable to travel due to difficulty because she is not denying him a right or disobeying him.[55]
- A wife is entitled to *nafaqah* even if she is in long term illness.
- A wife is entitled to *nafaqah* even if her husband is tied down with other debts.[56]
- A wife is entitled to *nafaqah* according to the needs of the family such that if a servant needs to be employed to help relieve the domestic duties, the husband must hire one out.[57]

لا تسترد النفقة التي دفعت للزوجة معجلاً لا بموت ولا طلاق سواء عجلها الزوج أو أبوه ولو كانت قائمة

[54] Ibid., art.161:

تجب النفقة للزوجة على زوجها ولو هي مقيمة في بيت أبيها ما لم يطالبها الزوج بالنقلة وتمتنع بغير حق

[55] Ibid., art:162:

تجب النفقة للزوجة ولو أبت أن تسافر مع زوجها فيما هو مسافة قصر أو فوقها أو منعت نفسها لاستيفاء ما تعورف تعجيله من المهر سواء كان قبل الدخول بها أو بعده

[56] Ibid., art:164:

إذا كان الزوج محبوساً ولو بدين عليه لزوجته فلا تسقط نفقتها وإن كان غير قادر على أدائه

[57] Ibid., art:165:

إذا كان الزوج موسراً وكان لامرأته خادمة تجب عليه نفقتها بقدر ما يكفيها على حسب العرف بشرط أن تكون الخادمة مملوكة لها ملكاً تاماً ومتفرغة لخدمتها لا شغل لها غيرها وإذا زفت إليه بخدم كثير استحقت نفقة الجميع عليه إن كان ذا يسار وإذا رزق أولاداً لا يكفيهم خادم واحد يفرض عليه نفقة خادمين أو أكثر على قدر حاجة أولاده

- A wife is entitled to *nafaqah* that is in accordance with her husband's change in financial circumstances, e.g. if he becomes wealthier, her *nafaqah* increases accordingly and if becomes less wealthy then her *nafaqah* decreases.[58]
- A wife is entitled to *nafaqah* when accompanying her husband on travels, trips and any place she is with him he if he decided to take her and even if she decided to take him.[59]
- A wife is entitled to *nafaqah* even if she is working because her own income does not cancel or replace her husband's obligation.
- A wife is entitled to *nafaqah* if she left her house become of unjust acts by the husband, e.g. physical abuse, hard threats, life endangered, etc.
- A wife is entitled to *nafaqah* even if she avoids sexual intercourse with her husband if he did not pay her dowry as she is objecting on the basis of a legal right.
- A divorce woman's expenses are paid by her relatives and not her ex-husband.

---

[58] Ibid., art:179:

النفقة المقدرة لا تبقى بحال واحدة بعد تقديرها بل تتغير تبعاً لتغير أحوال الزوجين بحيث لو قضى بنفقة الإعسار أو بنفقة اليسار بأيسر أحدهما أو أعسر تقدر نفقة الوسط وأن أيسر بعد إعسارها تتمم نفقة اليسار للمستقبل

[59] Ibid., art:168:

فإن سافر زوجها وأخذها معه فلها عليه نفقة الحضر ونفقة السفر ولوازمه وإن سافرت هي وأخذت زوجها معها فلها عليه نفقة الحضر لا نفقة السفر

- A divorced woman's expenses during her *'iddah period only* are paid for by the ex-husband.
- A marriage through an invalid marriage contract does not obligate *nafaqah* on the husband because the legal cause (*sabab*) for the marriage does not exist, i.e. actual possession of the wife.
- A wife is not entitled to *nafaqah* if she is imprisoned as a result of a debt or criminal charge because she has put herself in a position where her husband can no longer have contact or access to her by her own actions and not by his action.[60]
- A wife is not entitled to *nafaqah* if she disobeys her husband or leaves his house without his permission for the period she is like this because she is leaving confinement from him by her choice.[61] This is known as *nushuz* (disobedience to the husband).
- A wife is not entitled to *nafaqah* if she refuses to have any sexual intercourse with her husband without a valid reason because part of the marital right is to enjoy the wife.
- A wife is not entitled to *nafaqah* if she sets out to perform Hajj with a *ghayr mahram* person (father, brother, etc.) other than her husband.

---

[60] Ibid., art:170:

إذا حبست المرآة ولو في دين لا تقدر على إيفائه فلا يلزم زوجها نفقتها مدة حبسها إلا إذا كان هو الذي حبسها في دين له

[61] Ibid., art:171:

الناشزة وهي التي خالفت زوجها وخرجت من بيته بلا إذنه بغير وجه شرعي يسقط حقها في النفقة مدة نشوزها وإن كانت لها نفقة مفروضة متجمدة تسقط أيضاً بنشوزها

- A wife is not permitted to gain her *nafaqah* entitlements by selling off her husband's possessions or to rent out his property or benefit from what is not hers in the event that he was away or disappeared. A court cannot order that this be carried out either.[62]
- If the wife is a minor (*saghirah*) and no sexual intercourse took place, then she is not entitled to *nafaqah*.[63]
- If a husband is not physically present to provide *nafaqah* for his wife, then the court judge (*qadi*) can order him to pay her a fixed allowance (alimony) and he will be bound to that.
- If a husband actually fails to provide *nafaqah* for his wife, then the court judge (*qadi*) will not separate the two but will order the wife to take out a debt on the liability of her husband.
- If a husband is missing, gone for a long time or absent indefinitely, a *qadi* can also authorise the wife to take from her husband's wealth that which is sufficient for her *nafaqah*.[64]

---

[62] Ibid., art:195:

إذا كانت الوديعة أو المال الذي في بيت الزوج الغائب من غير جنس النفقة فليس للزوجة أن تبيع منه شيئاً في نفقة نفسها ولا للقاضي بيع شيء منه وتؤجر عقاراته ويصرف من أجرتها في نفقة المرآة

[63] Ibid., art:166:

إذا كانت الزوجة صغيرة لا تصلح للرجال، ولا تشتهي للوقاع ولو فيما دون الفرج فلا نفقة لها على زوجها إلا إذا أمسكها في بيته للاستئناس بها

[64] Ibid., art:196:

في كل موضع جاز للقاضي أن يقضي للمرآة بالنفقة من مال زوجها الغائب جاز لها أن تأخذ منه ما يكفيها بالمعروف من غير قضاء

Contemporary scenarios:

1. **Child benefit**: child benefit is paid from the benefits office which is part of the HMRC, i.e. the department responsible for social security. This is a state allowance and whoever they pay has ownership rights to the allowance. Whatever the woman receives in allowances for her and her children cannot be admitted as part of the husband's *nafaqah*. This is because any funds received by the wife external to her husband (e.g. gifts, inheritance, salary, etc.) are her own and cannot be counted as *nafaqah* by the husband. Whatever he provides of food, clothing and shelter is counted as *nafaqah* because it is from his wealth.

§4. Wali Amr ('Legal Guardian')

- The word "*wali*" comes from the root *w / l / y /* meaning 'friend' (opposite of enemy), 'friend of God', 'helper', 'assistant', 'representative' and 'guardian'.[65]

---

[65] al-Mawsili, *al-Ikhtiyar*, 3:117:

(باب الأولياء والأكفاء) شروع في بيان ما ليس بشرط لصحة النكاح عندنا وهو الولي وله معنى لغوي وفقهي وأصولي فالولي في اللغة خلاف العدو والولاية بالكسر السلطان والولاية النصرة، وقال سيبويه الولاية بالفتح المصدر والولاية بالكسر الاسم مثل الأمارة والنقابة؛ لأنه اسم لما توليته وقمت به فإذا أرادوا المصدر فتحوا كذا في الصحاح وفي الفقه البالغ العاقل الوارث، فخرج الصبي والمعتوه والكافر على المسلمة. وفي أصول الدين: هو العارف بالله تعالى وبأسمائه وصفاته حسبما يمكن، المواظب على الطاعات، المجتنب عن المعاصي، الغير المنهمك في الشهوات واللذات كما في شرح العقائد

- The legal guardian (*wali amr*) is from the "*'asabah*" (عصبة) which are for example the following (not necessarily in order):[66]

[a] Father.
[b] Great grandfather.
[c] Step father.
[d] Grandfather.
[e] Blood brother.
[f] Nephew.
[g] Uncle,
[n] etc...

- A *wali amr* has to be:

1. Male.
2. Mature (*baligh*).
3. Related.

- It is permissible that a *wali amr* be:

1. The Sultan/Khalifah.
2. The Judge (because he is an appointed official representing the Khalifah).[67]
3. The Imam of the Mosque.
4. A trustworthy Muslim man.
5. A sinful Muslim man (not ideal).

---

[66] Ibn 'Abidin, *Radd al-Muhtar*, 4:190.
[67] Ibid., 3:55:

(قوله وإمامة) دخل فيها القاضي المأذون بالتزويج لأنه نائب عن الإمام (قوله شاء أو أبى) احترز به عن ولاية الوكيل

→ This holds in scenarios where a woman is unduly
hindered in marrying the person of her choice by the family
member she appointed as her *wali amr*.

Related rulings:

- A woman does not require, legally speaking, a legal
  guardian (*wali amr*) as a condition of her marriage
  according to the Hanafis.[68]
- In some cases, the *wali amr* will have a right to
  block a marriage, e.g. in the case of unsuitability
  scenarios (*kafa'ah*).[69]
- If a woman marries herself to a person who is not her
  suitable match or equal (refer to the section on
  'Suitability' above), the marriage will not be valid
  according to one Hanafi position.[70]
- It is not allowed for the *wali amr* to force a woman
  to marry.[71]
- It is not allowed for the *wali amr* to use blackmail
  tactics to make a woman marry a man she does not
  want to.
- It is not allowed for the *wali amr* to take the dowry
  without the express permission of the woman.
- It is not allowed for a non-Muslim to be a *wali amr*
  for a Muslim girl (e.g. for a convert). She can choose

---

[68] Ibid., 3:56-57 and Qudri Paşa, *al-Ahkam al-Shar'iyyah*, art.52.
[69] Zafar Usmani, *I'la' al-Sunan*, 11:69.
[70] Ibid., 11:69.
[71] Ibid., 11:69-70. Ibn 'Abidin, *Radd al-Muhtar*, 3:58:

(قوله ولا تجبر البالغة) ولا الحر البالغ والمكاتب والمكاتبة ولو صغيرين ح عن القهستاني (قوله البكر)
أطلقها فشمل ما إذا كانت تزوجت قبل ذلك، وطلقت قبل زوال البكارة فتزوج كما تزوج الأبكار نص عليه في
الأصل بحر

the Imam of the Mosque or any trustworthy Muslim male (although technically, she does not even need a *wali amr* as per the Hanafi School).

- It is allowed for a *wali amr* to insist on the marriage of a young virgin girl or minor (boy or girl) without their permission.
- It is allowed for a *wali amr* to marry off two minors in marriage but the two people – when they reach maturity – have the choice to either continue with the marriage or annul it.
- It is not necessary that the *wali amr* conduct the marriage ceremony (*nikah*).
- It is allowed for a woman to change her *wali amr* if she feels her interests are being eroded without valid reason (e.g. blocking marriages on no valid Shariah grounds).
- It is allowed for a woman to be a *wali amr* according to the Hanafi School if there are no close male next of kin (i.e. relatives).
- It is allowed for the *wali amr* to take responsibility of ensuring the *mahr* is taken on behalf of the woman.

'Allamah al-Sindi commented:

إذا كان بين اثنين محبة فتلك المحبة لا يزيدها شيء من أنواع التعلقات بالتقربات ولا يديمها مثل تعلق النكاح، فلو كان بينهما نكاح مع تلك المحبة لكانت المحبة كل يوم بالازدياد والقوة

"...if there is love between two people, that love cannot be increased or made to last longer by anything like marriage. If there is marriage between them as well as that love, then the love they have will increase and grow stronger every day..." (*Hashiyah* on *hadith* #1847 of Tirmidhi's *Sunan*).

Chapter 3: "So, What Makes a Marriage?
Beyond the Legal Ingredients..."

———— Δ ————

§1. Aims of a Marriage in Islam

The marriage system constitutes the basic unit of the private life within the wider society.[72] Marriage is the system by which the relationship between a man and a woman is regulated. Islam sees marriage only meaningfully in this context. Subsequent to this relationship, other matters arise concerning both sides (e.g. parenthood, custody, etc.) which have to also be regulated. This system of marriage is detailed and defined and exists primarily to ensure that sex (procreation) secures the survival of the human species. This is the purpose of the procreation instinct. Thus, marriage is ultimately *generative* in its aims. It is the means by which the procreation instinct is satisfied and thus fulfils its teleology [cf. Q. 4:1; 7:189; 13:38; 16:32; 30:21; 52:45-46; 78:8].

Enjoyment and pleasure is intrinsic to procreation and inseparable from it but it is not its ultimate aim. Therefore, marriage is not just about pleasure and sexual enjoyment. Nevertheless, pleasure, enjoyment and physical gratification are all natural desires and therefore need to be met. Imam Ibn Qayyim al-Jawziyyah writes regarding sex:

"Concerning sexual relations, the Prophet's guidance (saw) is the best guidance whereby health may be preserved, pleasure and enjoyment found and it the purpose for which it

---

[72] al-Nabhani, *The Social System in Islam* (English, 3rd edition), pp.14-19.

was created realised, because sex was created for three basic purposes: [1] The preservation and propagation of the human race, until they reach the number of souls that Allah has decreed should be created in this world. [2] Expulsion of the fluid (semen) which may cause harm to the body if it is retained. [3] Fulfilling physical desires and enjoying physical pleasure. This alone is the feature that will be present in Paradise, because there will be no producing of offspring there, and no retention which needs to be relieved by ejaculation. The best doctors suggest that sex is one of the means of maintaining good health."[73]

وأما الجماع أو الباه، فكان هديه فيه – صلى الله عليه و سلم – أكمل هدي، يحفظ به الصحة، وتتم به اللذة وسرور النفس، ويحصل به مقاصده التي وضع لأجلها، فإن الجماع وضع في الأصل لثلاثة أمور هي مقاصده الأصلية :

أحدها : حفظ النسل ، ودوام النوع إلى أن تتكامل العدة التي قدر الله بروزها إلى هذا العالم. الثاني : إخراج الماء الذي يضر احتباسه واحتقانه بجملة البدن. الثالث : قضاء الوطر، ونيل اللذة، والتمتع بالنعمة، وهذه وحدها هي الفائدة التي في الجنة، إذ لا تناسل هناك، ولا احتقان يستفرغه الإنزال . وفضلاء الأطباء يرون أن الجماع من أحد أسباب حفظ الصحة

§2. It's not just about Sex

Yes, sex is important! Physical intimacy and romance is essential to enriching a marriage. Islam does not consider 'the flesh' as something bad. Islam embraces pleasure and enjoyment as long as it is within guidelines of the Sacred Law. This point of the importance of sex was not

---

[73] Ibn al-Qayyim, *al-Tibb al-Nabawi*, p.249.

lost the classical Muslim scholars. They composed detailed works on sexual etiquette that will surprise even the most progressive reader.[74] However, there are additional aspects to a relationship that can be just as fulfilling as sex – aspects that create *connectivity*. The Prophet is a paradigm of love, mercy and romance and many of his blessed actions reveal gentleness, care and attention as well as intimacy all necessary for the to be connectivity between spouses:

1. Loving words: The Prophet would often gaze lovingly in 'A'ishah's eyes and compliment her by saying: **'how white your eyes are!'**[75] He would also call her by endearing and intimate names like '*humayra*" (lit. 'the red one'; but here meaning beautiful and fair because the Arabs use 'red' to refer to something that is fair and white).[76]

---

[74] For basic references on Islamic sexual etiquette, see:

1. http://www.themodernreligion.com/misc/sex/sex-basic-fiqh.html
2. http://www.sunnipath.com/Library/Articles/AR00000214.aspx
3. http://www.livingislam.org/fiqhi/fiqha_e92.html#2
4. http://www.islamweb.net/emainpage/index.php?page=showfatwa&Option=FatwaId&Id=81556
5. http://islamqa.info/en/ref/5560

[75] See *Kitab al-Fawa'id* of Ibn al-Qayyim (#796):

عَنْ أَنَس بْنِ مَالِكٍ، أَنَّ النَّبِيَّ صَلَّى اللهُ عَلَيْهِ وَسَلَّمَ قَالَ لِعَائِشَةَ ذَاتَ يَوْمٍ: «مَا أَكْثَرَ بَيَاضَ عَيْنَيْكِ»

[76] See Ibn Majah, *Sunan* (#2474 = *Misbah al-Zujajah* of al-Busiri, 1:78):

عَنْ عَائِشَةَ، أَنَّهَا قَالَتْ: يَا رَسُولَ اللَّهِ مَا الشَّيْءُ الَّذِي لَا يَحِلُّ مَنْعُهُ؟ قَالَ: «الْمَاءُ، وَالْمِلْحُ، وَالنَّارُ» ، قَالَتْ: قُلْتُ: يَا رَسُولَ اللَّهِ هَذَا الْمَاءُ قَدْ عَرَفْنَاهُ، فَمَا بَالُ الْمِلْحِ وَالنَّارِ؟ قَالَ: «يَا حُمَيْرَاءُ مَنْ أَعْطَى نَارًا، فَكَأَنَّمَا تَصَدَّقَ بِجَمِيعِ مَا أَنْضَجَتْ تِلْكَ النَّارُ

يَا حميراء الخ قَالَ فِي النِّهَايَة الْحُمَيْرَاء تَصْغِير الْحَمْرَاء يُرِيد الْبَيْضَاء

Related rulings:

1. It is permitted to say romantic words to one's spouse.
2. It is permitted to use loving words and terms of endearment for one's spouse.
3. It is permitted to use romantic talk as part of foreplay.

2. Intimacy:[77] The Prophet would kiss his wives regularly – even while fasting –[78] and be intimate with them such as lying on their laps,[79] bathing together and eating from the same plate with them.[80]

---

[77] There is currently a course offered detailing the *ahkam shar'iyyah* (legal rulings) related to marital intimacy. See http://duha.org.uk/course/fiqh-of-marital-intimacy/ as well as my *Introducing the Fiqh of Marital Intimacy*.

[78] Bukhari, *Sahih* (#1106):

عَنْ عَائِشَةَ رَضِيَ اللهُ عَنْها: «أَنَّ النَّبِيَّ صَلَّى اللهُ عَلَيْهِ وَسَلَّمَ كَانَ يُقَبِّلُهَا وَهُوَ صَائِمٌ» فَسَكَتَ سَاعَةً، ثُمَّ قَالَ: نَعَمْ

[79] Bukhari, *Sahih* (#297):

عَائِشَةَ حَدَّثَتْهَا أَنَّ النَّبِيَّ صَلَّى اللهُ عَلَيْهِ وَسَلَّمَ: «كَانَ يَتَّكِئُ فِي حَجْرِي وَأَنَا حَائِضٌ، ثُمَّ يَقْرَأُ القُرْآنَ»

[80] Nasa'i, *Sunan* (#279):

قَالَ: سَمِعْتُ عَائِشَةَ رَضِيَ اللَّهُ عَنْهَا تَقُولُ: «كَانَ رَسُولُ اللَّهِ صَلَّى اللهُ عَلَيْهِ وَسَلَّمَ يُنَاوِلُنِي الْإِنَاءَ فَأَشْرَبُ مِنْهُ وَأَنَا حَائِضٌ، ثُمَّ أُعْطِيهِ فَيَتَحَرَّى مَوْضِعَ فَمِي فَيَضَعُهُ عَلَى فِيهِ»

Related rulings:

1. It is highly encouraged to be intimate with one's spouse.
2. It is encouraged to engage in intimate actions with one's spouse.
3. It is permitted to unrestrictedly kiss one's spouse, i.e. in every part.

3. Appearance: The Prophet used to admire and love good appearance in the believer and many of the companions incorporated this into their program of romance towards their spouses. Thus, Ibn 'Abbas would say:

"As my wife adorns herself for me, I adorn myself for her. I do not want to take all of my rights from her so that she will not take all of her rights from me because Allah, the Exalted, stated the following: {*And women shall have rights similar to the rights against them* [Q. 2:228]}..."[81]

Related rulings:

1. It is permitted to dress up for one's spouse.
2. It is permitted to adorn one's self for one's spouse.
3. It is permitted to make one's spouse feel wanted and desired.

---

[81] Ibn Abi Shaybah, *al-Musannaf* (#12263):

عَنِ ابْنِ عَبَّاسٍ قَالَ: " إِنِّي أُحِبُّ أَنْ أَتَزَيَّنَ لِلْمَرْأَةِ، كَمَا أُحِبُّ أَنْ تَتَزَيَّنَ لِي الْمَرْأَةُ، لِأَنَّ اللَّهَ تَعَالَى يَقُولُ: {وَلَهُنَّ مِثْلُ الَّذِي عَلَيْهِنَّ بِالْمَعْرُوفِ} [البقرة: 228]

§3. Marriage as Companionship

The relationship of marriage must be built on companionship (*suhbah*) in all respect and all aspects.[82] Thus, marriage ought to produce in each person repose and tranquillity.[83] A companionship can only be realized through mutual understanding, mutual love, mutual kindness and living[84] – 'mutual' being the operative word. Allah states this in several places within the Qur'an:

$$\text{﴿ هُوَ ٱلَّذِى خَلَقَكُم مِّن نَّفۡسٖ وَٰحِدَةٖ وَجَعَلَ مِنۡهَا زَوۡجَهَا}$$

$$\text{لِيَسۡكُنَ إِلَيۡهَاۖ فَلَمَّا تَغَشَّىٰهَا حَمَلَتۡ حَمۡلًا خَفِيفًا فَمَرَّتۡ بِهِۦۖ}$$

$$\text{فَلَمَّآ أَثۡقَلَت دَّعَوَا ٱللَّهَ رَبَّهُمَا لَئِنۡ ءَاتَيۡتَنَا صَٰلِحٗا لَّنَكُونَنَّ مِنَ}$$

$$\text{ٱلشَّٰكِرِينَ ﴿١٨٩﴾}$$

'It is He who created you from one soul and created from it its mate <u>that he might dwell in security with her.</u> And when he covers her, she carries a light burden and continues therein. And when it becomes heavy, they both invoke Allah, their Lord: "If You should give us a good [child], we will surely be among the grateful"...' (Q. 7:189).

- Allah describes the partnership between Adam and Hawa as one in which there is security, pleasure, serenity and tranquillity and not just a biological fulfilment.[85]

---

[82] al-Nabhani, *The Social System in Islam*, p.157.

[83] Ibid., p.157.

[84] Ibid., p.157.

[85] al-Qurtubi, *al-Jami' li-Ahkam al-Qur'an*, 7:302 comments on this verse:

وَمِنْ ءَايَتِهِۦٓ أَنْ خَلَقَ لَكُم مِّنْ أَنفُسِكُمْ أَزْوَٰجًا لِّتَسْكُنُوٓا۟ إِلَيْهَا وَجَعَلَ بَيْنَكُم مَّوَدَّةً وَرَحْمَةً إِنَّ فِى ذَٰلِكَ لَءَايَٰتٍ لِّقَوْمٍ يَتَفَكَّرُونَ ﴿٢١﴾

'And of His signs is that He created for you from
yourselves mates that you may find tranquility in them
and He placed between you affection and mercy. Indeed
in that are signs for a people who give thought' (Q.
30:21).

- Allah has made human beings with the natural
disposition to be with another. This disposition must
be expressed in a relationship that is built not only
on mutual love, mercy and kindness but refuge,
gentleness, security and tranquility.[86]

For there to be 'tranquility' (itmi'nan) between
spouses, a number of ingredients are essential. Five are
outlined below:

قوله تعالى: { هُوَ ٱلَّذِي خَلَقَكُم مِّن نَّفْسٍ وَاحِدَةٍ } قال جمهور المفسرين: المراد بالنفس الواحدة آدم. { وَجَعَلَ مِنْهَا زَوْجَهَا } يعني حوّاء. { لِيَسْكُنَ إِلَيْهَا } ليأنس بها ويطمئن،

[86] al-Suyuti in *Tafsir al-Jalalyn*, 2:95 writes:

{ وَمِنْ ءَايَتِهِ أَنْ خَلَقَ لَكُم مِّنْ أَنفُسِكُمْ أَزْوَاجاً } فخلقت حوّاء من ضلع آدم وسائر النساء من نطف الرجال والنساء { لِّتَسْكُنُوٓا۟ إِلَيْهَا } وتألفوها { وَجَعَلَ بَيْنَكُم } جميعا { مَّوَدَّةً وَرَحْمَةً إِنَّ فِى ذَٰلِكَ } المذكور { لَءَايَٰتٍ لِّقَوْمٍ يَتَفَكَّرُونَ } في صنع الله تعالى

1. Trust: The cornerstone of any type of relationship is trust. There must be a reciprocal belief and confidence as well as a conviction in the reliability of one partner towards the other. Both suspicion and negligence are destructive for a relationship: suspicion because it breeds anxiety, insecurity and negligence because it breeds carelessness. The Prophet emphatically forbade breaking trusts and characterized those who, for example, disclose secrets of others or break trusts as "the most evil of people"[87] and an act of "utmost treachery:"[88]

"Among the most evil of people before Allah on the Day of Resurrection will be a man who is intimate with a woman and she with him, then he spreads her secret..."

إن من أشر الناس عند الله منزلة يوم القيامة الرجل يفضي إلى المرأة وتفضي إليه ثم ينشر سرَّها

"One of the greatest [breach of] trusts before Allah on the Day of Resurrection will be a man who was intimate with his wife and she with him, then he spread her secret..."

إن من أعظم الأمانة عند الله يوم القيامة الرجل يفضي إلى امرأته وتفضي إليه ثم ينشر سرها

2. Managing expectations: Spouses have to reflect on what expectations they have or what they believe a person will be or ought to be. They have to manage expectations either by not being too rigid with ideals or by allowing room in the

---

[87] Muslim, *Sahih* (#1437).
[88] Muslim, *Sahih* (#1437).

relationship for things to develop and grow *over time*. No relationship is complete from the beginning; it undergoes a process. In Islam, marriage is not the termination of a relationship, i.e. the end product; it is the beginning – the journey stage.

3. Patience and support: Marriage can be difficult not just because of clear differences in personality or character of each person but because of external pressures such as work, family and environment that interfere or intrude on the relationship. These pressures can be overwhelming and overbearing which is why patience is paramount and supporting each other indispensable. One's spouse should be one's sanctuary; a place of refuge and respite from challenges and tests Allah has set down. Anas Ibn Malik reports that:

> "Safiyah was on a journey with the Prophet (saw). She was late so the Prophet (saw) received her while she was crying saying: 'you put me on a slow camel'. The Prophet (saw) wiped her tears with his own hands and tried his utmost to calm her down…"[89]

عَنْ أَنَسِ بْنِ مَالِكٍ قَالَ: كَانَتْ صَفِيَّةُ مَعَ رَسُولِ اللهِ صَلَّى اللهُ عَلَيْهِ وَسَلَّمَ فِي سَفَرٍ، وَكَانَ ذَلِكَ يَوْمَهَا فَأَبْطَأَتْ فِي الْمَسِيرِ، فَاسْتَقْبَلَهَا رَسُولُ اللهِ صَلَّى اللهُ عَلَيْهِ وَسَلَّمَ وَهِيَ تَبْكِي وَتَقُولُ: «حَمَلْتَنِي عَلَى بَعِيرٍ بَطِيءٍ، فَجَعَلَ رَسُولُ اللهِ صَلَّى اللهُ عَلَيْهِ وَسَلَّمَ يَمْسَحُ بِيَدَيْهِ عَيْنَيْهَا وَيُسْكِتُهَا

4. Communication and Understanding: spouses should know each other; they should come to understand aspects

---

[89] al-Bayhaqi, *Sunan al-Kubra* (#9117).

about their partner and learn what makes a person who they are and why they are the way they are; access to the inner thoughts or even behaviour patterns of one's spouse is therefore very important. Moreover communicating one's thoughts and feelings goes without saying; understanding stems from knowing something; understanding how one's spouse feels only stems from it being communicated – it cannot always be guessed or assumed. This helps manage and even minimize conflict or evident differences. The Prophet (saw) said to 'A'ishah – the mother of the believers:

'I know well when you are pleased or angry with me'. 'A'ishah replied: How do you know that? He said: **'when you are pleased with me you swear by saying: "By the God of Mohammad" but when you are angry you swear by saying: "By the God of Ibrahim".** She said: Messenger of Allah, you are right, I don't mention your name."[90]

عَنْ عَائِشَةَ رَضِيَ اللَّهُ عَنْهَا، قَالَتْ: قَالَ لِي رَسُولُ اللَّهِ صَلَّى اللهُ عَلَيْهِ وَسَلَّمَ: «إِنِّي لَأَعْلَمُ إِذَا كُنْتِ عَنِّي رَاضِيَةً، وَإِذَا كُنْتِ عَلَيَّ غَضْبَى» قَالَتْ: فَقُلْتُ: مِنْ أَيْنَ تَعْرِفُ ذَلِكَ؟ فَقَالَ: " أَمَّا إِذَا كُنْتِ عَنِّي رَاضِيَةً، فَإِنَّكِ تَقُولِينَ: لاَ وَرَبِّ مُحَمَّدٍ، وَإِذَا كُنْتِ عَلَيَّ غَضْبَى، قُلْتِ: لاَ وَرَبِّ إِبْرَاهِيمَ " قَالَتْ: قُلْتُ: أَجَلْ وَاللَّهِ يَا رَسُولَ اللَّهِ، مَا أَهْجُرُ إِلَّا اسْمَكَ

5. Roles: The Shariah has defined roles for both men and women, i.e. mandatory roles where division of labour is clearly laid out.[91] Men have the primary role of maintaining the financial stability of the house whereas the woman's paramount role is to build the home and raise the children. However, this does not entail that the roles cannot cross or

---

[90] Bukhari, *Sahih* (#5228).
[91] al-Nabhani, *The Social System in Islam*, pp.78-88 and cf. 89-111.

converge. There is no harm, for example, in the husband also taking ownership of the household chores and assisting his wife in that. And there is no harm in the wife also working. The Prophet would engage in household duties and assist in whatever help was required:

حدثنا آدم قال حدثنا شعبة قال حدثنا الحكم عن إبراهيم عن الأسود قال: سألت عائشة ما كان النبي صلى الله عليه و سلم يصنع في بيته؟ قالت كان يكون في مهنة أهله تعني خدمة أهله فإذا حضرت الصلاة خرج إلى الصلاة

"[…] al-Aswad said: I asked 'A'ishah what the Prophet would do in his house and she replied: He would be at the service of his family, i.e. helping his family; when the Prayer time entered he went out to pray."[92]

عَفَّانُ قَالَ مَهْدِيٌّ هِشَامُ بْنُ عُرْوَةَ عَنْ أَبِيهِ عَنْ عَائِشَةَ أَنَّهَا سُئِلَتْ مَا كَانَ رَسُولُ اللَّهِ صَلَّى اللَّهُ عَلَيْهِ وَسَلَّمَ يَعْمَلُ فِي بَيْتِهِ قَالَتْ كَانَ يَخِيطُ ثَوْبَهُ وَيَخْصِفُ نَعْلَهُ وَيَعْمَلُ مَا يَعْمَلُ الرِّجَالُ فِي بُيُوتِهِمْ

"[…] 'Urwah from his father who said when 'A'ishah was asked about what the Prophet (saw): he would sow his own clothes and stitch his own sandals and do whatever men did in the house…" [93]

Some important wider points to heed:

1. *Marriage is not just about ease and pleasure.* Why should we assume that? (cf. media portrayals of marriages as always exciting and fun). Allah definitely has not stated life is easy or free from

[92] Bukhari, *Sahih* (#5692).
[93] Ahmad, *al-Musnad* (#24927).

tests, hard responsibilities and exertion. So why should we expect marriage to be the same. Also, think about whether someone can build, develop or improve without ever being tested.

2. *Fighting the battle between your ears*. Marriage is not about pointing the finger, holding grudges, blaming or living in the past; one's own ego-self (*nafs*) can degrade and become worse even after marriage. If one believes they are faultless, perfect and never in the wrong then this is something highly detrimental for a loving relationship. A hard heart and a marriage do not go together.

3. *Love is a verb*. The difficulties of life like work, age, stress, *da'wah*, responsibilities, etc. will wear away the 'feel good' factor of marriage. Feelings of romance, passion and even happiness will fluctuate but real love is based on the pleasure of Allah and the strong commitment to honouring trusts Allah has put down 'for better or for worse'.

4. *Same method, same results*. Marriage is not about sinking into a mundane routine-ness; it is not just about coasting without any need for examination and assessment (cf. cultural perceptions of marriage as merely routine); minor changes, variations and creativity helps bring a difference and freshness to the relationship.

§4. The Dangers of Being Over-Legalistic

Islam has given rights to the husband and wife. These rights are varied and different. Islam has also laid down duties and obligations for both. These are also varied and different. This is one dimension of the relationship, i.e. knowing one's rights (what they can legally and religiously *have*) and knowing one's duties (what they must legally and religiously *do*). However, living life only in this dimension is extremely dangerous and results in a mechanized relationship devoid of human aspects such as love, mercy, passion, concern, care, understanding, pardon and other emotional co-ordinates evident from the life of the Prophet. Living a marriage only within the legal dimension does not correctly achieve 'companionship' that the Qur'an has created human marriage for. Some consequences of being over legalistic in a marriage are the following:

1. *Being inflexible*: unable to adapt to needs, circumstances and changes; unable to withstand differences in situations; unable to be resilient.

2. *Being inconsiderate*: becoming thoughtless; does not care; callous; lacking regard for the feelings of the spouse.

3. *Being immature*: lacking wisdom and intelligence; no developed sense or thinking.

4. *Being confrontational*: creating conflict and argumentative stances between each other; it turns difference into discord and disagreement into a clash.

The Prophet said:

خيركم خيركم لأهله وأنا خيركم لأهلي

"The Best of you is the one who is best to his family and I am the best of you to my family..."
(Tirmidhi, *Sunan* [#3895]).

Chapter 4: "Rights and Responsibilities: *I Ain't got a Scooby-Doo!*"

Islam has laid down rights and responsibilities for both the husband and the wife. These are not to be viewed from the angle of whether they are gender biased or unfair because the Legislator does not legislate a ruling on the basis of favouring one gender over another but rather as a solutions to particular problems. The Husband's rights and responsibilities and the wife's rights and responsibilities are mentioned in the Islamic evidences and a fulfilled marriage, in large part, is built upon knowledge of what one is *entitled* to and what one *must* do. Below is a list of rights and duties of spouses:

[1] Duties of the husband and rights of the wife:

1. *The dowry* (*mahr*): the money agreed before the marriage contract is concluded.

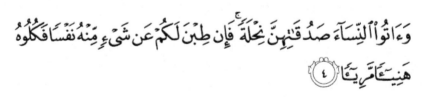

'And give the women [upon marriage] their [bridal] gifts graciously. But if they give up willingly to you anything of it, then take it in satisfaction and ease [Q. 4:4].'

2. *Support*: material maintenance; essential provisions for domestic and non-domestic matters (food, clothing, etc.).

۞ وَٱلْوَٰلِدَٰتُ يُرْضِعْنَ أَوْلَٰدَهُنَّ حَوْلَيْنِ كَامِلَيْنِ لِمَنْ أَرَادَ أَن يُتِمَّ ٱلرَّضَاعَةَ وَعَلَى ٱلْمَوْلُودِ لَهُ رِزْقُهُنَّ وَكِسْوَتُهُنَّ بِٱلْمَعْرُوفِ لَا تُكَلَّفُ نَفْسٌ إِلَّا وُسْعَهَا لَا تُضَآرَّ وَٰلِدَةٌ بِوَلَدِهَا وَلَا مَوْلُودٌ لَّهُ بِوَلَدِهِ وَعَلَى ٱلْوَارِثِ مِثْلُ ذَٰلِكَ فَإِنْ أَرَادَا فِصَالًا عَن تَرَاضٍ مِّنْهُمَا وَتَشَاوُرٍ فَلَا جُنَاحَ عَلَيْهِمَا وَإِنْ أَرَدتُّمْ أَن تَسْتَرْضِعُوٓا۟ أَوْلَٰدَكُمْ فَلَا جُنَاحَ عَلَيْكُمْ إِذَا سَلَّمْتُم مَّآ ءَاتَيْتُم بِٱلْمَعْرُوفِ وَٱتَّقُوا۟ ٱللَّهَ وَٱعْلَمُوٓا۟ أَنَّ ٱللَّهَ بِمَا تَعْمَلُونَ بَصِيرٌ ۝

'…Upon the father is the mothers' provision and their clothing according to what is acceptable. No person is charged with more than his capacity [Q.2:233].'

لِيُنفِقْ ذُو سَعَةٍ مِّن سَعَتِهِ وَمَن قُدِرَ عَلَيْهِ رِزْقُهُ فَلْيُنفِقْ مِمَّآ ءَاتَىٰهُ ٱللَّهُ لَا يُكَلِّفُ ٱللَّهُ نَفْسًا إِلَّا مَآ ءَاتَىٰهَا سَيَجْعَلُ ٱللَّهُ بَعْدَ عُسْرٍ يُسْرًا ۝

'Let a man of wealth spend from his wealth, and he whose provision is restricted - let him spend from what Allah has given him [Q.65:7].'

3. *Kind and proper treatment*: kind words, affection, the best behaviour and proper manners.

يَـٰٓأَيُّهَا ٱلَّذِينَ ءَامَنُواْ لَا يَحِلُّ لَكُمْ أَن تَرِثُواْ ٱلنِّسَآءَ كَرْهَاً وَلَا تَعْضُلُوهُنَّ لِتَذْهَبُواْ بِبَعْضِ مَآ ءَاتَيْتُمُوهُنَّ إِلَّآ أَن يَأْتِينَ بِفَـٰحِشَةٍ مُّبَيِّنَةٍ وَعَاشِرُوهُنَّ بِٱلْمَعْرُوفِ فَإِن كَرِهْتُمُوهُنَّ فَعَسَىٰٓ أَن تَكْرَهُواْ شَيْئاً وَيَجْعَلَ ٱللَّهُ فِيهِ خَيْرَاً كَثِيرَاً ﴿١٩﴾

'O you who have believed, it is not lawful for you to inherit women by compulsion. And do not make difficulties for them in order to take [back] part of what you gave them unless they commit a clear immorality. <u>And live with them in kindness</u>. For if you dislike them - perhaps you dislike a thing and Allah makes therein much good [Q. 4:19].'

وَٱلْمُطَلَّقَـٰتُ يَتَرَبَّصْنَ بِأَنفُسِهِنَّ ثَلَـٰثَةَ قُرُوٓءٍ وَلَا يَحِلُّ لَهُنَّ أَن يَكْتُمْنَ مَا خَلَقَ ٱللَّهُ فِىٓ أَرْحَامِهِنَّ إِن كُنَّ يُؤْمِنَّ بِٱللَّهِ وَٱلْيَوْمِ ٱلْأَخِرِ وَبُعُولَتُهُنَّ أَحَقُّ بِرَدِّهِنَّ فِى ذَٰلِكَ إِنْ أَرَادُوٓاْ إِصْلَـٰحاً وَلَهُنَّ مِثْلُ ٱلَّذِى عَلَيْهِنَّ بِٱلْمَعْرُوفِ وَلِلرِّجَالِ عَلَيْهِنَّ دَرَجَةٌ وَٱللَّهُ عَزِيزٌ حَكِيمٌ ﴿٢٢٨﴾

'Divorced women remain in waiting for three periods, and it is not lawful for them to conceal what Allah has created in their wombs if they believe in Allah and the Last Day. And their husbands have more right to take them back in this [period] if they want reconciliation. <u>And due to the wives is similar to what is expected of them, according to what is reasonable.</u> But the men have a degree over them [in responsibility and authority]. And Allah is Exalted in Might and Wise [Q. 2:228].'

- The Prophet said regarding treatment of women: **"and treat them in the best way..."**[94]

... استوصوا بالنساء

4. *Marital relations*: sex, intimacy, love and affection.

- Ibn 'Abidin comments on mutual rights of intimacy:

ونقله ط وأقره والظاهر أن المراد ليس لها إجبار على ذلك لا بمعنى أنه لا يحل لها إذا
منعها منه لأن من أحكام النكاح حل استمتاع كل منهما بالآخر، نعم له وطؤها جبرا إذا
امتنعت بلا مانع شرعي وليس لها إجباره على الوطء بعدما وطئها مرة، وإن وجب عليه ديانة
أحيانا على ما سيأتي تأمل

"[...] and one of the rulings of marriage is the permissibility of each spouse to sexually enjoy the other..."[95]

5. *Not to be ill-treated*: safe from physical or mental abuse.

استوصوا بالنساء خيرا فإنهن عندكم عوانٍ ليس تملكون منهن شيئا غير ذلك إلا أن يأتين
بفاحشة مبينة فإن فعلن فاهجروهن في المضاجع واضربوهن ضربا غير مبرح فإن أطعنكم

---

[94] Bukhari, *Sahih* (#3153).
[95] Ibn 'Abidin, *Radd al-Muhtar*, 3:4.

فلا تبغوا عليهن سبيلا إن لكم من نسائكم حقا ولنسائكم عليكم حقا فأما حقكم على
نسائكم فلا يوطئن فرشكم من تكرهون ولا يأذن في بيوتكم لمن تكرهون ألا وحقهن عليكم
أن تحسنوا إليهن في كسوتهن وطعامهن.

"Treat women kindly, for they are like captives among but you have no other power over them than that; if they are guilty of open lewdness, then refuse to share their beds, and discipline them, but not severely. But if they return to obedience, [then] do not seek means [of annoyance] against them. You have rights over your women and your women have rights over you. Your rights over your women are that they should not let anyone whom you dislike sit on your bed and they should not let anyone whom you dislike enter your house. Their rights over you are that you should feed and clothe them well…"[96]

6. *Privacy*: either in a separate room, house or dwelling.

أَسْكِنُوهُنَّ مِنْ حَيْثُ سَكَنتُم مِّن وُجْدِكُمْ وَلَا تُضَارُّوهُنَّ لِتُضَيِّقُوا۟ عَلَيْهِنَّ
وَإِن كُنَّ أُو۟لَٰتِ حَمْلٍ فَأَنفِقُوا۟ عَلَيْهِنَّ حَتَّىٰ يَضَعْنَ حَمْلَهُنَّ فَإِنْ أَرْضَعْنَ
لَكُمْ فَـَٔاتُوهُنَّ أُجُورَهُنَّ وَأْتَمِرُوا۟ بَيْنَكُم بِمَعْرُوفٍ وَإِن تَعَاسَرْتُمْ فَسَتُرْضِعُ
لَهُۥٓ أُخْرَىٰ ﴿٦﴾

'Lodge them [in a section] of where you dwell out of your means and do not harm them in order to oppress them. And if they should be pregnant, then spend on them until they

---

[96] Tirmidhi, *Sunan* (#1163).

give birth. And if they breastfeed for you, then give them their payment and confer among yourselves in the acceptable way; but if you are in discord, then there may breastfeed for the father another woman [Q. 65:6].'

7. *Justice*: fairness of treatment especially if she is a co-wife.

وَإِنْ خِفْتُمْ أَلَّا تُقْسِطُوا فِى ٱلْيَتَـٰمَىٰ فَٱنكِحُوا مَا طَابَ لَكُم مِّنَ ٱلنِّسَآءِ مَثْنَىٰ

وَثُلَـٰثَ وَرُبَـٰعَ ۖ فَإِنْ خِفْتُمْ أَلَّا تَعْدِلُوا فَوَٰحِدَةً أَوْ مَا مَلَكَتْ أَيْمَـٰنُكُمْ ۚ ذَٰلِكَ أَدْنَىٰ

أَلَّا تَعُولُوا ۝ ٣

'And if you fear that you will not deal justly with the orphan girls, then marry those that please you of [other] women, two or three or four. But if you fear that you will not be just, then [marry only] one or those your right hand possesses. That is more suitable that you may not incline [to injustice] [Q. 4:3].'

8. *To be taught her religion*: her religious obligations such as purity, prayer, fasting, buying and selling, etc. for which she will be accountable before Allah.

يَـٰٓأَيُّهَا ٱلَّذِينَ ءَامَنُوا قُوٓا أَنفُسَكُمْ وَأَهْلِيكُمْ نَارًا وَقُودُهَا ٱلنَّاسُ

وَٱلْحِجَارَةُ عَلَيْهَا مَلَـٰٓئِكَةٌ غِلَاظٌ شِدَادٌ لَّا يَعْصُونَ ٱللَّهَ مَآ أَمَرَهُمْ

وَيَفْعَلُونَ مَا يُؤْمَرُونَ ۝ ٦

'O you who have believed, protect yourselves and your families from a Fire whose fuel is people and stones, over which are [appointed] angels, harsh and severe; they do not disobey Allah in what He commands them but do what they are commanded [Q.66:6].'

- Ibn Kathir in his commentary on this verse says:

وقال قتادة : تأمرهم بطاعة الله، وتنهاهم عن معصية الله، وأن تقوم عليهم بأمر الله، وتأمرهم به، وتساعدهم عليه، فإذا رأيتَ لله معصية قذعتهم عنها (كففتهم)، وزجرتهم عنها .وهكذا قال الضحاك ومقاتل : حق المسلم أن يعلم أهله من قرابته وإمائه وعبيده ما فرض الله عليهم وما نهاهم الله عنه .

"Qatadah said: you should command them to obey Allah, and forbid them to disobey Allah; you should be in charge of them in accordance with the command of Allah, and instruct them to follow the commands of Allah, and help them to do so. If you see any act of disobedience towards Allah, then stop them from doing it and rebuke them for that. This was also the view of al-Dahhak and Muqatil: that the duty of the Muslim is to teach his family, including his relatives and his slaves, that which Allah has enjoined upon them and that which He has forbidden them..."[97]

9. *Defence of her honour*: protecting her lineage, name and family from slander, defamation and accusations.

---

[97] Ibn Kathir, *Tafsir al-Qur'an al-'Azim*, 4:392.

[2] Duties of the wife and rights of the husband:

1. *Being head of the household*: respecting his authority and position.

اَلرِّجَالُ قَوَّامُونَ عَلَى ٱلنِّسَآءِ بِمَا فَضَّلَ ٱللَّهُ بَعْضَهُمْ عَلَى بَعْضٍ وَبِمَآ أَنفَقُواْ مِنْ أَمْوَٰلِهِمْ فَٱلصَّٰلِحَٰتُ قَٰنِتَٰتٌ حَٰفِظَٰتٌ لِّلْغَيْبِ بِمَا حَفِظَ ٱللَّهُ وَٱلَّٰتِي تَخَافُونَ نُشُوزَهُنَّ فَعِظُوهُنَّ وَٱهْجُرُوهُنَّ فِي ٱلْمَضَاجِعِ وَٱضْرِبُوهُنَّ فَإِنْ أَطَعْنَكُمْ فَلَا تَبْغُواْ عَلَيْهِنَّ سَبِيلًا إِنَّ ٱللَّهَ كَانَ عَلِيًّا كَبِيرًا ۝

'Men are in charge of women by [right of] what Allah has given one over the other and what they spend [for maintenance] from their wealth. So righteous women are devoutly obedient, guarding in [the husband's] absence what Allah would have them guard. But those [wives] from whom you fear arrogance - [first] advise them; [then if they persist], forsake them in bed; and [finally], strike them. But if they obey you [once more], seek no means against them. Indeed, Allah is ever Exalted and Grand [Q. 4:34].'

- Ibn Kathir writes:

وقال علي بن أبي طلحة عن ابن عباس { الرجال قوامون على النساء } يعني : أمراء
عليهن، أي : تطيعه فيما أمرها الله به من طاعته، وطاعته أن تكون محسنة لأهله حافظة
لماله . وكذا قال مقاتل والسدي والضحاك

"'Ali ibn Abi Talhah said, narrating from Ibn
'Abbas: {*Men are the protectors and maintainers of
women*} means: they are in charge of them, i.e., she should
obey him in matters of obedience that Allah has enjoined
upon her and obey him by treating his family well and
taking care of his wealth. This was the view of Muqatil, al-
Suddi and al-Dahhak..."[98]

2. *Obedience*: To be obeyed in all that is not
   disobedience to Allah.

- Ibn Taymiyyah comments on the parameters of
  obedience to the husband and serving him:

"She is obliged to serve her husband according to
what is reasonable among people of similar standing. That
varies according to circumstances: the way in which a
Bedouin woman serves [her husband] will not be like the
way of a town-dweller, and the way of a strong woman will
not be like the way of a weak woman..."[99]

وتجب خدمة زوجها بالمعروف من مثلها لمثله ويتنوع ذلك بتنوع الأحوال فخدمة البدوية
ليست كخدمة القروية وخدمة القوية ليست كخدمة الضعيفة .

---

[98] Ibn Kathir, *Tafsir al-Qur'an al-'Azim*, 1:492.
[99] Ibn Taymiyyah, *al-Fatawa al-Kubra*, 4:561.

3. *Marital relations*: love, affection and intimacy.

- Ibn 'Abidin comments on mutual rights of intimacy:

ونقله ط وأقره والظاهر أن المراد ليس لها إجبار على ذلك لا بمعنى أنه لا يحل لها إذا منعها منه لأن من أحكام النكاح حل استمتاع كل منهما بالآخر، نعم له وطؤها جبرا إذا امتنعت بلا مانع شرعي وليس لها إجباره على الوطء بعدما وطئها مرة، وإن وجب عليه ديانة أحيانا على ما سيأتي تأمل

"[...] and one of the rulings of marriage is the permissibility of each spouse to sexually enjoy the other..."[100]

- Abu Hurayrah narrates from the Prophet that he said: **"When a man calls his wife to his bed and she refuses and he went to sleep angry with her, the angels will curse her until morning."**[101]

إذا دعا الرجل امرأته إلى فراشه فأبت فبات غضبان عليها لعنتها الملائكة حتى تصبح

4. That she not allow anyone in the house of whom he disapproves.

- The Prophet stated: **"It is not permitted for a wife to fast while her husband is present without his consent and she should not let anyone enter his house without his permission."**[102]

---

[100] Ibn 'Abidin, *Radd al-Muhtar*, 3:4.
[101] Bukhari, *Sahih* (#3065).
[102] Bukhari, *Sahih* (#4899).

لا يحل للمرأة أن تصوم وزوجها شاهد إلا بإذنه، ولا تأذن في بيته إلا بإذنه

The Prophet also stated: "You have rights over your women and your women have rights over you. <u>Your rights over your women are that they should not let anyone whom you dislike sit on your bed and they should not let anyone whom you dislike enter your house.</u> Their rights over you are that you should feed and clothe them well..."[103]

إن لكم من نسائكم حقا ولنسائكم عليكم حقا فأما حقكم على نسائكم فلا يوطئن فرشكم من تكرهون ولا يأذن في بيوتكم لمن تكرهون ألا وحقهن عليكم أن تحسنوا إليهن في كسوتهن وطعامهن.

5. *That she not leave the house without his permission*: because through marriage, the husband has right of exclusive location with his wife in his own home.

6. *That she keeps well his house (difference of opinion)*: such as domestic duties of cleaning, cooking and general chores.

7. *To be thanked for his efforts*: acknowledgement, appreciation, reciprocal kindness as well as accepting that support and affirmation from the husband's efforts is a gift from Allah.

---

[103] Tirmidhi, *Sunan* (#1163).

8. *That she not fast a voluntary fast without his permission*: as her husband may want to enjoy time with her (e.g. a meal, etc.) or even intimate relations.

- The Prophet stated: **"It is not permitted for a wife to fast while her husband is present without his consent and she should not let anyone enter his house without his permission."**[104]

لا يحل للمرأة أن تصوم وزوجها شاهد إلا بإذنه، ولا تأذن في بيته إلا بإذنه

[3] Mutual duties/rights of spouses:

1. The Right to enjoy each other (intimacy).

2. The right to inherit from each other.

3. The right of conformation of their lineage (to know their children).

Related rulings:

1. *Cooking for husband*: If a woman is from an upper class family or she does not customarily do the cooking or cleaning, then it is an obligation on the husband to provide services for her so that the food is prepared and ready to eat. If however she does not come from such a family then it is mandatory for her to perform the domestic duties of her house herself including cooking and cleaning.[105]

---

[104] Bukhari, *Sahih* (#4899).
[105] Ibn 'Abidin, *Radd al-Muhtar*, 3:579:

2. *Looking after in-laws*: Strictly speaking, it is not mandatory for a woman to serve and be on call for her in-laws – especially her parent in-laws. The same is the case for a man. In the case of serving her-laws, if this makes the husband happy, she should willingly and happily do that as that would be a virtuous act but the husband cannot force her.

3. *Equality between co-wives*: A man must be fair and show qualitative equality with his wives. The Shariah has stipulated the areas that a husband must be equitable and they are the following areas:

[1] Wealth and provisions: material support and needs.

[2] Clothing.

[3] Shelter: a place to reside, room or house.

[4] The night time: sex, intimacy and affection.

[5] Affection and socialising: visiting relatives, outdoor engagements, social functions, etc.

(امتنعت المرأة) من الطحن والخبز (إن كانت ممن لا تخدم) أو كان بها علة (فعليه أن يأتيها بطعام مهيا وإلا) بأن كانت ممن تخدم نفسها وتقدر على ذلك (لا) يجب عليه ولا يجوز لها أخذ الأجرة على ذلك لوجوبه عليها ديانة ولو شريفة؛ لأنه – عليه الصلاة والسلام – قسم الأعمال بين علي وفاطمة، فجعل أعمال الخارج على علي – رضي الله عنه – والداخل على فاطمة – رضي الله عنها – مع أنها سيدة نساء العالمين

4. *Separate dwelling*: It is legally required for a husband to provide a full residence for his spouse. However, if he is unable to provide a separate place of residence, he must provide a separated room for her which is a private room unhindered by any other member of the family.[106]

5. *Right to work*: A wife has the permission from the Shariah to work. However, if the husband disapproves because he wants his wife to raise the children at home then this is permitted for him. The underlying reason being that one of the legal consequences of a marriage is that the husband owns the right of the wife to be with him exclusively in the confines of his home.[107]

6. *Right to visit parents*: Although strictly speaking a husband can prevent his wife from leaving the house, it is not permitted for him to bar his wife from visiting her parents at least once a week – especially if they are unable to visit her or to allow her to visit her parents according to what is customarily considered or 'reasonable'. He also cannot prevent her from visiting her *mahram* relatives at least once a

---

[106] M. Qudri Paşa, *al-Ahkam al-Shar'iyyah*, 1:422:

وكما تجب النفقة و الكسوة علي الزوج لزوجته تجب عليه السكني لها

al-Kasani states in *al-Bada'i' al-Sana'i* as quoted in Ibn 'Abidin's *Radd al-Muhtar*, 3:601:

لو اراد ان يسكنها مع ضرتها او مع احمائها كامه و اختهو بنته فابت <u>فعليه ان يسكنها في منزل منفرد</u> لان ابائها دليل الاذي و الضرر

[107] al-Kasani, *al-Bada'i' al-Sana'i*, 2:231.

year or according to what is customarily considered 'reasonable'. Failure to allow her can result in a Shariah court injunction to impose this right.[108]

7. *Medical expenses*: The jurists are divided over whether or not medical expenses fall under the category of obligatory maintenance (*nafaqah*). Classical Hanafi *fuqaha'* deem it not to be mandatory as it was not considered a necessity then but a luxury. Contemporary jurists deem medical expenses as a necessity and so under the husband's duty for expenses. They also deem it to fall under

---

[108] Ibn 'Abidin, *Radd al-Muhtar*, 3:602-603:

(قوله على ما اختاره في الاختيار) الذي رأيته في الاختيار شرح المختار : هكذا قيل لا يمنعها من الخروج إلى الوالدين وقيل يمنع ولا يمنعهما من الدخول إليها في كل جمعة وغيرهم من الأقارب في كل سنة هو المختار . ا ه فقوله هو المختار مقابله القول بالشهر في دخول المحارم كما أفاده في الدرر والفتح، نعم ما ذكره الشارح اختاره في فتح القدير حيث قال : وعن أبي يوسف في النوادر تقييد خروجها بأن لا يقدرا على إتيانها، فإن قدرا لا تذهب وهو حسن، وقد اختار بعض المشايخ منعها من الخروج إليهما وأشار إلى نقله في شرح المختار . والحق الأخذ بقول أبي يوسف إذا كان الأبوان بالصفة التي ذكرت، وإلا ينبغي أن يأذن لها في زيارتهما في الحين بعد الحين على قدر متعارف، أما في كل جمعة فهو بعيد، فإن في كثرة الخروج فتح باب الفتنة خصوصا إذا كانت شابة والزوج من ذوي الهيئات، بخلاف خروج الأبوين فإنه أيسر . ا ه .

وهذا ترجيح منه لخلاف ما ذكر في البحر أنه الصحيح المفتى به من أنها تخرج للوالدين في كل جمعة بإذنه وبدونه ، وللمحارم في كل سنة مرة بإذنه :وبدونه (قوله زمنا) أي مريضا مرضا طويلا (قوله فعليها تعاهده) أي بقدر احتياجه إليها، وهذا إذا لم يكن له من يقوم عليه كما قيده في الخانية (قوله ولو كافرا) لأن ذلك من المصاحبة بالمعروف المأمور بها) قوله وإن أبى الزوج) لرجحان حق الوالد، وهل لها النفقة؟ الظاهر لا وإن كانت خارجة من بيته بحق كما لو خرجت لفرض الحج (قوله في كل جمعة) هذا هو الصحيح، خلافا لمن قال له المنع من الدخول معللا بأن المنزل ملكه، وله حق المنع من دخول ملكه دون القيام على باب الدار، ولمن قال لا منع من الدخول بل من القرار؛ لأن الفتنة في المكث وطول الكلام، أفاده في البحر .

treating women honourably and kindly from the
verse: {*and live with them honourably*...[4:19]}.[109]

---

[109] Dr. W. al-Zuhayli writes in *al-Fiqh al-Islami wa Adillatuhu*, 10:7380:

قرر فقهاء المذاهب الأربعة أن الزوج لا يجب عليه أجور التداوي للمرأة المريضة من أجرة طبيب وحاجم
وفاصد وثمن دواء، وإنما تكون النفقة في مالها إن كان لها مال، وإن لم يكن لها مال وجبت النفقة على من
تلزمه نفقتها [كالابن والأب ومن يرثها من أقاربها] لأن التداوي لحفظ أصل الجسم، فلا يجب على مستحق
المنفعة، كعمارة الدار المستأجرة، تجب على المالك لا على المستأجر ... ويظهر لي أن المداواة لم تكن في
الماضي حاجة أساسية، فلا يحتاج الإنسان غالبا إلى العلاج، لأنه يلتزم قواعد الصحة والوقاية، فاجتهاد
الفقهاء مبني على عرف قائم في عصرهم . أما الآن فقد أصبحت الحاجة إلى العلاج كالحاجة إلى الطعام
والغذاء، بل أهم؛ لأن المريض يفضل غالبا ما يتداوى به على كل شيء، وهل يمكنه تناول الطعام وهو يشكو
ويتوجع من الآلام والأوجاع التي تبرح به وتجهده وتهدده بالموت؟! لذا فإني أرى وجوب نفقة الدواء على
الزوج كغيرها من النفقات الضرورية ... وهل من حسن العشرة أن يستمتع الزوج بزوجته حال الصحة، ثم
يردها إلى أهلها لمعالجتها حال المرض؟!

The *fuqaha'* of the four *madhhabs* stated that the husband is not obliged
to pay for the medical expenses of the sick wife, such as the fees of the
doctor and cupper, or the cost of the medicine, rather those expenses
should be paid from her wealth if she has any wealth. If she does not
have any wealth then it must be paid by one who is obliged to spend on
her [such as a son, father or relative who would inherit from her],
because medicine is aimed at preserving the body, so it is not required of
the one who benefits from it. This is like maintenance of a building for
the tenant – it is required from the landlord, not the tenant. It seems to
me that in the past, medical treatment was not a basic need, so people
did not usually need medical treatment, because they followed health
rules and precautions. So the *ijtihad* of the *fuqaha'* was based on the
prevalent custom during their era. But now, the need for medical
treatment has become like the need for food and nourishment, and even
more important, because the sick person usually gives his medicine
precedence over everything else. Can he eat when he is suffering pain
which causes extreme anguish and exhausts him and threatens him with
death? Hence, I think that medical expenses are obligatory upon the
husband like all other necessary expenses. Is it kind treatment for the
husband to enjoy his wife when she is healthy, then to send her back to
her family for them to treat her when she is sick? See
http://islamqa.info/en/ref/83815

Chapter 5: "Tackling Common Marriage Scenarios: *Fiqh in Application*"

——————— Θ ———————

§1. Marriage Scenarios

Below are a dozen or so common marriage scenarios with their Islamic rulings. Each case is always context sensitive and situation specific and therefore demands further deliberations, consultations and advice with relevant persons if a ruling is being sought.

1] Just not attracted to him!

- X does not find Y attractive enough to marry them where 'attractive' could cover physical qualities and personality traits.

- **Answer:**

    1. No obligation to marry.
    2. No need to feel guilty for declining a marriage offer.
    3. Attraction is important.
    4. Compatibility is important.
    5. It is permissible to marry a person for h/her physical beauty, status or assets – however, piety is far better a quality for grounding a relationship.[110]

------

[110] See Ibn 'Allan quoting al-Rafi'i in *Dalil al-Falihin li-Turuq Riyad al-Salihin*, 3:228 that although it is permitted to marry someone purely on their looks, only basing a marriage on this is not wise:

2] Older brother first!

- X cannot marry Y because X has an older brother who is not yet ready to marry.

- **Answer**:

  1. Be patient.
  2. Be sensitive.
  3. Be respectful.
  4. Turn to Allah.
  5. Always think of making parents happy.
  6. <u>Explain the Shariah rulings on priority</u>: a possible slide into an illicit relationship is given priority to address and solve over a cultural

---

قال الرافعي في المجلس الثالث عشر من أماليه: يرغب في النكاح لفوائد دينية ودنيوية، والفوائد المتعلقة بمطلق النكاح تحصل بنكاح أيّ امرأة كانت، ثم قال: فمن الدواعي القوية إليه الجمال، وقد نهى عن تزوّج المرأة الحسناء، وليس المراد النهي عن رعاية الجمال على الإطلاق، ألا ترى أنه قد أمر بنظر المخطوبة ليكون النكاح عن موافقة الطبع، ولكنه محمول على ما إذا كان القصد مجرد الحسن واكتفي به عن سائر الخصال، أو على الحسن التام البارع

al-Ghazzali says as quoted in *Irshad al-Sari Sharh Sahih al-Bukhari* by al-Qasatallani, 8:22-23 that looks is a valid consideration but a more deeper appreciation lies with religious considerations in a potential spouse:

وقال الغزالي في الإحياء: وليس أمره —صَلَّى اللَّهُ عَلَيْهِ وَسَلَّمَ— بمراعاة الدين نهيًا عن مراعاة الجمال ولا أمرًا بالإضراب عنه وإنما هو نهي عن مراعاته مجردًا عن الدين فإن الجمال في غالب الأمر يرغب الجاهل في النكاح دون التفات إلى الدين ولا نظر إليه فوقع النهي عن هذا. قال: وأمر النبي —صَلَّى اللَّهُ عَلَيْهِ وَسَلَّمَ— لمن يريد التزوج بالنظر إلى الخطوبة يدل على مراعاة الجمال إذ النظر لا يفيد معرفة الدين، وإنما يعرف به الجمال أو القبح

custom of elders marrying first.[111] Fear of sin takes priority over mere customary practice.

7. Family consultation, talks and collaborative efforts with a scholar are required to address specific situations/scenarios.

3] Bengali can't marry a Pakistani!

- X (a Bengali) wants to marry Y (a Pakistani) but families are opposed.

- **Answer**:

1. Be patient.
2. Turn to Allah.
3. Ponder carefully on the situation.
4. Understand the idea of mutual compatibility (*kufu'*) as a valid Shariah notion for many scholars. [112]

---

[111] See Tirmidhi, *Sunan*, 1:238: From Ali that the Prophet (saw) said to him: **"O Ali, there are three things which should not be delayed: the prayer when its time is due, the funeral when it is ready, and marrying off an unmarried woman when there is a suitable match for her..."**

حَدَّثَنَا قُتَيْبَةُ، قَالَ: حَدَّثَنَا عَبْدُ اللهِ بْنُ وَهْبٍ، عَنْ سَعِيدِ بْنِ عَبْدِ اللهِ الجُهَنِيِّ، عَنْ مُحَمَّدِ بْنِ عُمَرَ بْنِ عَلِيِّ بْنِ أَبِي طَالِبٍ، عَنْ أَبِيهِ، عَنْ عَلِيِّ بْنِ أَبِي طَالِبٍ، أَنَّ النَّبِيَّ صَلَّى اللَّهُ عَلَيْهِ وَسَلَّمَ قَالَ لَهُ: يَا عَلِيُّ، ثَلَاثٌ لاَ تُؤَخِّرْهَا: الصَّلَاةُ إِذَا آنَتْ، وَالجَنَازَةُ إِذَا حَضَرَتْ، وَالأَيِّمُ إِذَا وَجَدْتَ لَهَا كُفْئًا

[112] In *Tanwir al-Absar* (= *Radd al-Muhtar* of Ibn 'Abidin, 4:194) it states:

قال في تنوير الأبصار: الكفاءة معتبرة من جانبه لا من جانبها؛ وقال في الدر المختار: (من جانبه) أي الرجل لأن الشريفة تأبى أن تكون فراشا للدنيء ولذا (لا) تعتبر (من جانبها) لأن الزوج مستفرش فلا تغيظه دناءة الفراش وهذا عند الكل في الصحيح؛ وقال ابن عابدين في حاشيته: أي يعتبر أن يكون الرجل مكافئا

5. Always think of making parents happy.
6. There are no Shariah impediments to one heritage marrying into another heritage (mixed heritage marriages).

4] Can't marry her – she's *older*!

- X (man) wants to marry Y (woman) but Y is much older.

- **Answer**:

1. No harm in marrying an older girl/woman.
2. No reason to feel guilt or cave in to any social/cultural stigma.

لها في الأوصاف الآتية بأن لا يكون دونها فيها، ولا تعتبر من جانبها بأن تكون مكافئة له فيها بل فيها بل يجوز أن تكون دونه فيها (قوله ولذا لا تعتبر) تعليل للمفهوم، وهو أن الشريف لا يأبى أن يكون مستفرشا للدنيئة كالأمة والكتابية لأن ذلك لا يعد عارا في حقه بل في حقها لأن النكاح رق للمرأة والزوج مالك

In *Durr al-Mukhtar* (= *Radd al-Muhtar* of Ibn 'Abidin, 4:152) it has:

قال في الدر المختار: (ويفتى) في غير الكفء (بعدم جوازه أصلا) وهو المختار للفتوى (لفساد الزمان)؛ و قال ابن عابدين رحمه الله: وهذا إذا كان لها ولي لم يرض به قبل العقد، فلا يفيد الرضا بعده بحر وأما إذا لم يكن لها ولي فهو صحيح نافذ مطلقا اتفاقا كما يأتي الخ ... وقول البحر : لم يرض به يشمل ما إذا لم يعلم أصلا فلا يلزم التصريح بعدم الرضا بل السكوت منه لا يكون رضا كما ذكرناه فلا بد حينئذ لصحة العقد من رضاه صريحا، وعليه فلو سكت قبله ثم رضي بعده لا يفيد فليتأمل (قوله وهو المختار للفتوى) وقال شمس الأئمة وهذا أقرب إلى الاحتياط كذا في تصحيح العلامة قاسم لأنه ليس كل ولي يحسن المرافعة والخصومة ولا كل قاض يعدل، ولو أحسن الولي وعدل القاضي فقد يترك أنفة للتردد على أبواب الحكام، واستثقالا لنفس الخصومات فيتقرر الضرر فكان منعه دفعا له فتح

3. It is an action our beloved Prophet did (cf. Khadijah being 40 years old [ra] and he only 25).[113]

5] Breaking off an engagement

- X has been proposed to by Y but Y realises something in X that is not acceptable and thus causes the engagement to breakdown.

- **Answer**:

1. Being sensitive to the marriage process is highly important.
2. If there are genuine and valid reasons, it would be permitted to break off the engagement (e.g. incompatibility issues, etc.).[114]

---

[113] Ibn Kathir relates from Ibn Hisham: "Ibn Hisham states that the age of the Messenger of Allah (saw) when he married Khadijah was twenty-five years as told to me by a number of scholars..." See *al-Bidayah wa'l-Nihayah*, 2:295:

قَالَ ابْنُ هِشَامٍ: وَكَانَ عُمُرُ رَسُولِ اللَّهِ صَلَّى اللَّهُ عَلَيْهِ وَسَلَّمَ حِينَ تَزَوَّجَ خَدِيجَةَ خَمْسًا وَعِشْرِينَ سَنَةً فِيمَا حَدَّثَنِي غَيْرُ وَاحِدٍ مِنْ أَهْلِ الْعِلْمِ، مِنْهُمْ أَبُو عَمْرٍو الْمَدَنِيُّ. وَقَالَ يَعْقُوبُ بْنُ سُفْيَانَ كَتَبْتُ عَنْ إبراهيم بن المنذر حدثني عمر بن أبي بكر المؤملي حَدَّثَنِي غَيْرُ وَاحِدٍ أَنَّ عَمْرَو بْنَ أَسَدٍ زَوَّجَ خَدِيجَةَ مِنْ رَسُولِ اللَّهِ صَلَّى اللَّهُ عَلَيْهِ وَسَلَّمَ وَعُمْرُهُ خَمْسًا وَعِشْرِينَ سَنَةً وَقُرَيْشٌ تَبْنِي الْكَعْبَةَ

[114] See M. Qadri Paşa, *al-Ahkam al-Shar'iyyah fi 'l-Ahwal al-Shakhsiyyah*, 1:34: "[...] at that time, the one proposing can revoke his proposal..."

وحينئذ فللخاطب الرجوع عن المخطوبة

6] Woman becomes Muslim but husband remains non-Muslim

- A Muslim woman A becomes Muslim but her non-Muslim husband B does not accept Islam. Is the marriage still marriage?

- **Answer**:

1. Be sensitive to the situation.
2. Each case is specific.
3. Be aware of the social, emotional and religious consequences of the situation.
4. If the woman embraces Islam in a <u>Muslim</u> territory (*dar al-Islam*), Islam will be presented to the husband by the Qadi (judge) and if he refuses, the Qadi will issue a decree of separation which will be considered an irrevocable *talaq*.[115]
5. If the woman embraces Islam in a <u>non-Muslim</u> territory (*dar al-harb*) and her husband refuses to accept Islam, then she will wait three menstrual cycles and an automatic separation will take place and it will be considered an irrevocable *talaq*.[116]

---

[115] al-Marghinani, *al-Hidayah*, 2:346:

و اذا اسلمت المراة و زوجها كافر عرض القاضي عليه الاسلام, فان اسلم فهي امراته وان ابي فرق القاضي بينهماوكان ذالك طلاقا عند ابي حنيفة رحمه الله

[116] al-Bukhari, *al-Muhit al-Burhani*, 4:200:

و ان اسلم احد الزوجين فى دار الحرب فان الفرقة تقف على مضي ثلاث حيض فاذا مضت وقعت الفرقة....و لانقضاء ثلاث حيض أثر فى وقوع الفرقة بالطلاق

7] Temporary Marriages.

- X marries Y with the intention of later divorcing her or marries for only a period of time.

- **Answer:**

1. It is not permitted to set a time limit on marriage.[117]
2. Mut'ah marriages are not lawful.
3. Temporary marriages are not lawful.
4. Sham marriages are not permitted
5. Convenience marriages (*misyar*) are highly discouraged.

8] But the first wife doesn't even know!

- X marries a second wife Y without the first wife knowing.

- **Answer:**

1. A husband ought to be sensitive and understanding.
2. Being given a Shariah permission does not mean one exercises it with utmost immaturity and insensitivity.
3. Emotional sensitivities of the first wife are very important (e.g. self-esteem, worth, dignity, etc.).

---

[117] Ibn 'Abidin, *Radd al-Muhtar*, 3:51:

(وبطل نكاح متعة ومؤقت) وإن جهلت المدة أو طالت في الأصح وليس منه ما لو نكحها على أن يطلقها بعد شهر أو نوى مكثه معها مدة

4. A husband must understand marriage is about issues of trust, fidelity and confidence; secret second marriages break this.
5. It is legally permitted to marry a second wife even if it upsets the first wife – how ever this does not mean it is appropriate (think about lying and deception).
6. Failure to be just with both wives is a cause of immense consequences in the Hereafter.[118]

9] Every four months??

- Husband has been away from the wife for more than four months and the wife is finding it difficult.
- **Answer**:

    1. Husband must understand his wife's needs – emotional and ***PHYSICAL***.
    2. It is required that the husband return to his wife within **four months** as it is her right to have marital intimacy with him.[119]

---

[118] The Prophet is reported to have said: "**Anyone who has two wives and he cannot fulfill their rights equally and justly, shall be raised on the Day of Judgment in a condition that one of his shoulders will be drooping down...**" See al-Tabrizi's *Mishkat al-Masabih*, 6:304 with the commentary of al-Tibi (= *al-Kashif 'an Haqa'iq al-Sunan*):

عن أبى هريرة عن النبى –صلى الله عليه وسلم– قال « إذا كان عند الرجل امرأتان فلم يعدل بينهما جاء يوم القيامة وشقه ساقط

[119] Ibn 'Abidin, *Radd al-Muhtar*, 3:203:

(قوله ولا يبلغ مدة الإيلاء) تقدم عن الفتح التعبير بقوله ويجب أن لا يبلغ إلخ.

3. A husband must seek the permission of his wife if he needs or wants to stay beyond four months otherwise arrangements have to be made by the husband to either bring his wife over to where he is or he return to her.
4. The wife has the right to forfeit her right of marital intimacy every four months.

10] Love marriage

- X has been in love with Y for a long time and now wants to marry her.

- **Answer**:

1. Love before marriage is unislamic.
2. Love *through* marriage is the Islamic stance.[120]
3. Western perceptions of what a relationship should be based on have influenced the general Muslim collective consciousness (effects of Hollywood, Bollywood, etc.).

وظاهره أنه منقول، لكن ذكر قبله في مقدار الدور أنه لا ينبغي أن يطلق له مقدار مدة الإيلاء وهو أربعة أشهر، فهذا بحث منه كما سيذكره الشارح فالظاهر أن ما هنا مبني على هذا البحث تأمل، ثم قوله وهو أربعة يفيد أن المراد إيلاء الحرة، ويؤيد ذلك أن عمر رضي الله تعالى عنه لما سمع في الليل امرأة تقول : فوالله لولا الله تخشى عواقبه لزحزح من هذا السرير جوانبه فسأل عنها فإذا زوجها في الجهاد ، فسأل بنته حفصة : كم تصبر المرأة عن الرجل : فقالت أربعة أشهر، فأمر أمراء الأجناد أن لا يتخلف المتزوج عن أهله أكثر منها، ولو لم يكن في هذه المدة زيادة مضارة بها لما شرع الله تعالى الفراق بالإيلاء فيها .

[120] The Prophet said: **"There is nothing that creates more love than marriage..."** Ibn Majah, *Sunan* (#1847):

لم ير للمتحابين مثل النكاح

4. Love before a marriage does not guarantee a stable marriage.

11] Marrying a Christian or a Jew

- X (male) wants to marry a Christian or a Jewish woman.

Answer:

1. All factors should be considered (e.g. how strong is the husband islamically; his upbringing' the fact that there will be non-Muslim in-Laws, etc.).
2. Marriage is about securing holistic serenity in this world and the next.
3. It is permissible no marry a Christian and a Jew as long as they are not polytheists.[121]

12] Marrying secretly

- X marries Y secretly without telling anyone but with 2 witnesses.

Answer:

1. Marrying without parent's blessing is sinful.

---

[121] al-Mawsili, *al-Ikhtiyar li-Ta'lil al-Mukhtar*, 3:100:

(ويجوز تزويج الكتابيات) لقوله تعالى : والمحصنات من الذين أوتوا الكتاب من قبلكم [المائدة : 5]

والذمية والحربية سواء لإطلاق النص

2. Marriage should begin on a positive footing with blessings.
3. Marriage is, strictly, legal if witnesses are present but strongly discouraged.[122]

13] Marrying infertile women

- X marries an infertile woman Y but later regrets it.

- **Answer**:

1. Marrying infertile women is permitted.[123]
2. Marriage is one of the most serious commitments made before Allah so should not be taken lightly.
3. It is permitted for a man to marry a second wife if his first wife is unable to have children but all this must be done with sensitivity and maturity.

14] *Halalah* Marriage

- Woman Y wants to get back with her first husband X who divorced her 3 times.

- **Answer**:

---

[122] al-Quduri, *al-Mukhtasar*, pp.149-150:

النكاح ينعقد بالايجاب والقبول بلفظين يعبر بهما عن الماضي او يعبر باحدهما عن الماضي والاخر عن المستقبل... و لا ينعقد نكاح المسلمين الا بحضور شاهدين حرين بالغين عاقلين مسلمين او رجل وامراتين

[123] Abdul Haqq al-Haqqani, *al-Fatawa al-Haqqaniyyah*, 4:328.

1. If a woman was divorced by her first husband but wants to get back with him, then the Shariah route is that she must <u>marry</u> another man, <u>consummate</u> that marriage and be <u>divorced</u> by her second husband – however and whichever way that happens.[124]

15] Forced Marriage

- Person X was forced to marry person Y.

- **Answer**:

1. A human being is an agent for h/herself. They are permitted to choose whoever they want to marry.[125]
2. Forced marriages are not acceptable in Islam because offer and acceptance is required for the marriage to be valid.
3. No-one should have to endure a forced marriage.

---

[124] Ibn 'Abidin, *Radd al-Muhtar*, 5:51. See the section on 'Halalah' below for details.

[125] Ibn al-Humam, *Fath al-Qadir*, 3:256-259:

وينعقد نكاح الحرة العاقلة البالغة برضاها (وإن لم يعقد عليها ولي بكرا كانت أو ثيبا (عند أبي حنيفة وأبي يوسف (رحمهما الله (في ظاهر الرواية . وعن أبي يوسف (رحمه الله (أنه لا ينعقد إلا بولي . وعند محمد ينعقد وقوفا) وقال مالك والشافعيرحمهما الله لا ينعقد النكاح بعبارة النساء أصلا لأن النكاح يراد لمقاصده والتفويض إليهن مخل بها، إلا أن محمدا رحمه الله يقول : يرتفع الخلل بإجازة الولي ووجه الجواز أنها تصرفت في خالص حقها وهي من أهله لكونها عاقلة مميزة ولهذا كان لها التصرف في المال ولها اختيار الأزواج، وإنما يطالب الولي بالتزويج كي لا تنسب إلى الوقاحة، ثم في ظاهر الرواية لا فرق بين الكفء وغير الكفء ولكن للولي الاعتراض في غير الكفء. وعن أبي حنيفة وأبي يوسف رحمهما الله أنه لا يجوز في غير الكفء لأن كم من واقع لا يرفع . ويروى رجوع محمد إلى قولهما

4. However, if no-one forced a person to accept a marriage, even though they did not really want to marry that person, the marriage, strictly speaking, will be valid if it was accepted.

5. If marriage by compulsion and duress occurred, and this is proven through a Shariah court or tribunal, then an order of separation will be decreed and a discretionary punishment will be administered to the legal guardian or those involved.

——*PART TWO*

Chapter 6: Divorce Outlines

Chapter 7: Divorce types and Categories

Chapter 8: Divorce scenarios.

Chapter 9: Child Custody

Chapter 10: Dispelling Misconceptions

Chapter 6: "The Dreaded 'D' Word: *Outlines on Divorce*"

——————— Δ ———————

§1. Divorce: Preliminary Points

1. The Arabic word for 'divorce' is "*talaq*" (طلاق/ root: *t / l / q*) and means: 'to be loosened from a bond'; 'to be divorced'; 'to be separated from one's spouse'.[126]
2. Divorce is one of the most detested outcomes in the eyes of Allah.[127]
3. Divorce has drastic consequences and is an extremely serious matter in Islam and so must be treated with the utmost seriousness and gravity.[128]

———————————————

[126] E. W. Lane, *Arabic-English Lexicon*, Book 1, pp.1871-1872. In al-Mawsili, *al-Ikhtiyar*, 3:161, it states: "Linguistically it means freeing someone from a bond...in the Shariah it means 'being freed from the marriage bond'..."

وهو في اللغة : إزالة القيد والتخلية، تقول : أطلقت إبلي وأطلقت أسيري . وفي الشرع : إزالة النكاح الذي هو قيد معنى

[127] The narration regarding this is: **"The most detested thing to Allah is divorce"**. see Abu Dawud, *Sunan* (#2178):

أبغض الحلال إلى الله الطلاق

[128] For some basic references on divorce, see:

1. http://www.islamweb.net/emainpage/index.php?page=articles&id=92752
2. http://en.wikipedia.org/wiki/Divorce_(Islamic)
3. http://islamqa.info/en/cat/343
4. http://princeomaralkhattab.wordpress.com/category/fiqh-of-love-marriage-divorce/

4. Despite its gravity, divorce is a practical solution for a real situation. If two people just do not get along and cannot reconcile their differences then the option of separation – mutual parting – is open and this has specific rulings related to it.

§2. Causes of Divorce

There are a number of general <u>causes</u> of divorce. Some of these causes are listed below:

1. Misunderstanding.
2. Irreconcilable differences.
3. Pressure (e.g. family, work, social and career).
4. Changes in priority (e.g. career vs. family)
5. Abuse (physical, sexual and psychological).
6. Infidelity (e.g. cheating, dishonesty).
7. Poor communication.

Some causes of divorce within a specifically Muslim context of marriage are the following:

1. **Abuse**: this can be physical, sexual and psychological.

2. **Ignorance**: lack of knowledge of the Shariah rulings of divorce, e.g. pronouncing *talaq* unknowingly.

3. **Ideas**: social precepts, e.g. freedom, fun, etc.

---

5. http://www.islamographic.com/gallery/the-fiqh-of-divorce/

4. **Injustice**: this can be in the case of unfulfilled rights, e.g. spouses not fulfilling their Shariah obligations.

5. **Interference**: e.g. family meddling or in-law pressures.

§3. Valid Grounds for Divorce

- There are Shariah grounds for divorce and they include the following:

1. **Lack of *nafaqa***: Inability or refusal of the husband to financially support his wife (even if she happens to be rich, it is still the full responsibility of the husband to maintain her).[129]

2. **Abuse**: mistreatment of the wife (which includes beating and swearing, cursing and attempting to force her to do wrong).[130] This also extends to emotional and verbal forms of abuse and is severely punishable by law.[131]

---

[129] Although there are conditions here. The divorce decree will not be immediate because generally Hanafi jurists do not see financial difficulties as grounds for divorce because she can borrow on behalf of her husband. See al-Marghinani, *al-Hidayah*, 2:41.

[130] Qudri Paşa, *al-Ahkam al-Shar'iyyah*, art.209: "[…] and he has not permitted in origin to beat her in a depraved manner even if he thinks there is a reason or right for it…"

يباح للزوج تأديب المرآة تأديباً خفيفاً على كل معصية لم يرد في شأنها حد مقدر

ولا يجوز له أصلاً أن يضربها ضرباً فاحشاً ولو بحق

[131] Ibid., art.211:

3. **Impotence**: lack of libido or any other illness that prevents the husband from fulfilling the wife's sexual needs (in recognition of the wife's legitimate instinctive needs; cf. also castration).[132]

4. **Medical grounds**: Incurable, repulsive diseases in the husband like leprosy (or AIDS/HIV according to the contemporary scholars).

5. **Insanity**: i.e. mental and/or behavioural disorders in the husband or extreme abnormal behaviour, e.g. suicidal thoughts, psychopathic tendencies, etc.

6. **Desertion**: Extended absence, imprisonment or desertion of the husband.[133]

إذا اشتكت المرآة نشوز زوجها وضربه إياها ضرباً فاحشاً ولو بحق وثبت ذلك عليه بالبينة يعزر

[132] al-Marghinani, *al-Hidayah*, 2:404:

وإذا تشاق الزوجان وخافا أن لا يقيما حدود الله فلا بأس بأن تفتدي نفسها منه بمال يخلعها به لقوله تعالى { فلا جناح عليهما فيما افتدت به } فإذا فعلا ذلك وقع بالخلع تطليقة بائنة ولزمها المال لقوله عليه الصلاة والسلام الخلع تطليقة بائنة

[133] The early ruling in the Hanafi School was that a woman would need to wait until her husband would become around 120 years before she could remarry (as it would be deemed impossible for him to live beyond this time). The ruling was also that she had to wait until she reached 90 years of age after which she would be free to marry. However, due to the immense hardship in following this ruling, the Hanafi scholars ruled that adoption of the Maliki position would be valid which states that if a woman's spouse is missing (*mafqud*) for more than 4 years, she is permitted to marry someone else. See Ibn 'Abidin, *Radd al-Muhtar*, 4:295:

7. **Deception**: The husband deceiving and concealing information regarding himself at the time of marriage (e.g. secretly married to someone, has children but denies the claim, etc.).[134]

{قوله : خلافا لمالك} فإن عنده تعتد زوجة المفقود عدة الوفاة بعد مضي أربع سنين، وهو مذهب الشافعي القديم وأما الميراث فمذهبهما كمذهبنا في التقدير بتسعين سنة، أو الرجوع إلى رأي الحاكم

"It is stated in *al-Bazzaziyyah*: the *fatwa* that is issued in our times is the opinion of Malik. And al-Zahidi has stated that: some of our companions issue the *fatwa* based on the Maliki opinion due to necessity…"

وقد قال في البزازية : الفتوى في زماننا على قول مالك . وقال الزاهدي كان بعض أصحابنا يفتون به للضرورة

[134] al-Haskafi, *Durr al-Mukhtar*: 3:501:

(ولو تراضيا) أي العنين وزوجته (على النكاح) ثانيا (بعد التفريق صح) وله شق رتق أمته وكذا زوجته، وهل تجبر؟ الظاهر : نعم، لأن التسليم الواجب عليها لا يمكنه بدونه نهر .

قلت :وأفاد البهنسي أنها لو تزوجته على أنه حر، أو سني، أو قادر على المهر والنفقة فبان بخلافه، أو على أنه فلان بن فلان فإذا هو لقيط، أو ابن زنا كان لها الخيار فليحفظ.

Ibn 'Abidin, *Radd al-Muhtar*, 3:501-502:

(قوله : وكذا زوجته) أي له شق رتقها، لكن هذه العبارة غير منقولة وإنما المنقول قولهم في تعليل عدم الخيار بعيب الرتق لإمكان شقه، وهذا يدل على أن له ذلك ولذا قال في البحر بعد نقله التعليل المذكور، ولكن ما رأيت هل يشق جبرا أم لا قوله: (لأن التسليم الواجب إلخ) فيه أنه لا يلزم من وجوبه ارتكاب هذه المشقة، فقد سقط القيام في الصلاة للمشقة وسقط الصوم عن المرضع إذا خافت على نفسها أو ولدها، ونظائره كثيرة . وقد يفرق بأن هذا واجب له مطالب من العباد ط قوله : (لها الخيار) أي لعدم الكفاءة . واعترضه بعض مشايخ مشايخنا بأن الخيار للعصبة .

قلت : وهو موافق لما ذكره الشارح أول باب الكفاءة من أنها حق الولي لا حق المرأة لكن حققنا هناك أن الكفاءة حقهما، ونقلنا عن الظهيرية : لو انتسب الزوج لها نسبا غير نسبه فإن ظهر دونه وهو ليس بكفء

8. **Irreconcilability**: The relationship becoming severely damaged, in that there is a lot of hatred between the spouses and it is impossible for them to live a peaceful life.[135]

9. **Incest**: where persons unlawful for one another under Shariah law form a relationship together – whether civil or via a marriage contract.

10. **Apostasy**: a woman's marriage is automatically annulled with her husband if he leaves Islam (i.e. he becomes *murtadd*).[136]

11. **Ideological differences**: this can include differences in theological tenets or if one of the spouses is openly heretical.[137]

فحق الفسخ ثابت للكل، وإن كان كفؤا فحق الفسخ لها دون الأولياء، وإن كان ما ظهر فوق ما أخبر فلا فسخ لأحد. وعن الثاني أن لها الفسخ لأنها عسى تعجز عن المقام معه وتمامه هناك، لكن ظهر لي الآن أن ثبوت حق الفسخ لها للتغرير لا لعدم الكفاءة بدليل أنه لو ظهر كفؤا يثبت لها حق الفسخ لأنه غرها، ولا يثبت للأولياء لأن التغرير لم يحصل لهم، وحقهم في الكفاءة، وهي موجودة، وعليه فلا يلزم من ثبوت الخيار لها في هذه المسائل ظهوره غير كفء، والله سبحانه أعلم.

[135] Adapted from Mufti Ibn Adam al-Kawthari's "What Can the Wife Do if the Husband Refuses to Divorce Her?" at http://www.daruliftaa.com

[136] al-Marghinani, *al-Hidayah*, 1:461:

اعلم أن تصرفات المرتد على أقسام: نافذ بالاتفاق كالاستيلاد والطلاق، لأنه لا يفتقر إلى حقيقة الملك وتمام الولاية. وباطل بالاتفاق كالنكاح والذبيحة لأنه يعتمد الملة ولا ملة له. وموقوف بالاتفاق كالمفاوضة

[137] See al-Haskafi, al-*Durr al-Muntaqa* (on the margins of *Majma' al-Anhur*), 1:463-464.

§4. The Process of Divorce

Allah states in the Qur'an 65:1-5:

يَـٰٓأَيُّهَا ٱلنَّبِىُّ إِذَا طَلَّقْتُمُ ٱلنِّسَآءَ فَطَلِّقُوهُنَّ لِعِدَّتِهِنَّ وَأَحْصُوا۟ ٱلْعِدَّةَ
وَٱتَّقُوا۟ ٱللَّهَ رَبَّكُمْ لَا تُخْرِجُوهُنَّ مِنۢ بُيُوتِهِنَّ وَلَا
يَخْرُجْنَ إِلَّآ أَن يَأْتِينَ بِفَـٰحِشَةٍ مُّبَيِّنَةٍ وَتِلْكَ حُدُودُ ٱللَّهِ وَمَن
يَتَعَدَّ حُدُودَ ٱللَّهِ فَقَدْ ظَلَمَ نَفْسَهُ لَا تَدْرِى لَعَلَّ ٱللَّهَ يُحْدِثُ بَعْدَ
ذَٰلِكَ أَمْرًا ﴿١﴾

فَإِذَا بَلَغْنَ أَجَلَهُنَّ فَأَمْسِكُوهُنَّ بِمَعْرُوفٍ أَوْ فَارِقُوهُنَّ بِمَعْرُوفٍ
وَأَشْهِدُوا۟ ذَوَىْ عَدْلٍ مِّنكُمْ وَأَقِيمُوا۟ ٱلشَّهَـٰدَةَ لِلَّهِ ذَٰلِكُمْ
يُوعَظُ بِهِۦ مَن كَانَ يُؤْمِنُ بِٱللَّهِ وَٱلْيَوْمِ ٱلْءَاخِرِ وَمَن يَتَّقِ ٱللَّهَ يَجْعَل
لَّهُۥ مَخْرَجًا ﴿٢﴾

وَيَرْزُقْهُ مِنْ حَيْثُ لَا يَحْتَسِبُ وَمَن يَتَوَكَّلْ عَلَى ٱللَّهِ فَهُوَ حَسْبُهُۥٓ إِنَّ ٱللَّهَ
بَـٰلِغُ أَمْرِهِۦ قَدْ جَعَلَ ٱللَّهُ لِكُلِّ شَىْءٍ قَدْرًا ﴿٣﴾

وَٱلَّٰٓـِٔى يَئِسْنَ مِنَ ٱلْمَحِيضِ مِن نِّسَآئِكُمْ إِنِ ٱرْتَبْتُمْ فَعِدَّتُهُنَّ ثَلَٰثَةُ
أَشْهُرٍ وَٱلَّٰٓـِٔى لَمْ يَحِضْنَ وَأُولَٰتُ ٱلْأَحْمَالِ أَجَلُهُنَّ أَن يَضَعْنَ حَمْلَهُنَّ
وَمَن يَتَّقِ ٱللَّهَ يَجْعَل لَّهُۥ مِنْ أَمْرِهِۦ يُسْرًا ۝

ذَٰلِكَ أَمْرُ ٱللَّهِ أَنزَلَهُۥٓ إِلَيْكُمْ وَمَن يَتَّقِ ٱللَّهَ يُكَفِّرْ عَنْهُ سَيِّـَٔاتِهِۦ وَيُعْظِمْ لَهُۥٓ
أَجْرًا ۝

Translation:

{*O Prophet, when you [Muslims] divorce women, divorce them for [the commencement of] their waiting period and keep count of the waiting period and fear Allah, your Lord. Do not turn them out of their [husbands'] houses, nor should they [themselves] leave [during that period] otherwise they are committing a clear immorality. And those are the limits [set by] Allah. And whoever transgresses the limits of Allah has certainly wronged himself. You know not; perhaps Allah will bring about after that a [different] matter. /*

And when they have [nearly] fulfilled their term, either retain them according to acceptable terms or part with them according to acceptable terms. And bring to witness two just men from among you and establish the testimony for [the acceptance of] Allah. That is instructed to whoever should believe in Allah and the Last day. And whoever fears Allah - He will make for him a way out. /

And will provide for him from where he does not expect. And whoever relies upon Allah - then He is sufficient for him. Indeed, Allah will accomplish His purpose. Allah has already set for everything a [decreed] extent. /

And those who no longer expect menstruation among your women - if you doubt, then their period is three months, and [also for] those who have not menstruated. And for those who are pregnant, their term is until they give birth. And whoever fears Allah - He will make for him of his matter ease. / That is the command of Allah, which He has sent down to you; and whoever fears Allah - He will remove for him his misdeeds and make great for him his reward.}

- The basic process of a divorce *extra-judicial* is the following:

Step One: Seek reliable help from pious, wise, knowledgeable and experienced individuals like scholars, elders and professional mediators as they will advise properly, accordingly and with seriousness.

Step Two: seek reconciliation of differences through arbitration or mediation. It may be that in this stage, the couple reconcile differences or tensions and give the marriage another chance.

Step Three: if step two fails and there is no possibility of reconciliation, then the husband should issue one *talaq* ('pronounced divorce') and have it documented in the presence of witnesses.

Step Four: part amicably attending to any legal obligations post-divorce (e.g. custody, returning belongings, respecting one another, etc.).

Throughout the separation process, the couples should have, wherever and whenever possible, the following:

1. Mutual understanding.
2. Mutual sensitivity.
3. Fear of Allah.
4. Observance of Shariah rules.
5. Compassion.
6. Thankfulness to Allah.

Chapter 7: "Finding Our Way through the *Fiqh* of Divorce: *Elements to Consider and Understand*"

——————— Ξ ———————

§1. *'Iddah* Period (The waiting Period)

After a pronouncement of *talaq* by the husband, a woman enters what is called a 'waiting period' or "*'iddah*" (عِدَّة) in Arabic. It is from the root verb ' / *d* / *d* / which means to 'to count', 'to compute', 'to calculate' and 'to reckon'.[138] In legal terms, it refers to the mandatory time period a woman enters when her husband issues a divorce to her. The Islamic rulings pertaining to the *'iddah* are intricate and vary given the situation and condition of the woman and will be outlined below.[139] The wisdom behind the *'iddah* as explained by many Islamic scholars and commentators is:

> Some of these are: 1) making sure that she is not pregnant, so that there would be no confusion on who the father of the child is if the woman were to remarry and get pregnant right away; 2) to help couples, families and communities understand the gravity and sanctity of marriage; 3) in cases of divorce, the waiting period provides time for reconciliation and reconsideration, particularly if the divorce

---

[138] Lane, *Arabic-English Lexicon*, Bk.1, p.1969.

[139] Ibid., Book.1, p.1970. In *al-Fatawa al-Hindiyyah*, 1:526 it has: "[and *'iddah*] refers to the known waiting period necessary for a woman to observe after her marriage has dissolved whether actually or not..."

هي انتظار مدة معلومة يلزم المرأة بعد زوال النكاح حقيقة أو شبهة

took place on the insistence of the husband and
4) as an expression of grief on the passing of
the deceased husband.[140]

- The *'iddah* system of rules is a thus a way to safeguard the woman's protection and dignified exit from a marriage. The husband must see to the well-being, residence and condition of his ex-wife because he cannot mistreat her or discard her however he pleases.

- The length of the waiting period depends on the specific circumstances in question, based on the following:

1. **Three complete <u>menstrual</u> cycles**: for a divorced woman who undergoes menstruation and is not pregnant;[141]

2. **Three <u>lunar</u> months**: for a divorced woman in menopause (i.e. when she stops menstruating);[142]

---

[140] Umm Khaleel, "The Rulings and Wisdom of Idda" at
http://spa.qibla.com/issue_view.asp?HD=1&ID=13284&CATE=239
[141] al-Kasani, *al-Bada'i' al-Sana'i'*, 3:193:

فَأَمَّا عِدَّةُ الْأَقْرَاءِ فَإِنْ كَانَتْ الْمَرْأَةُ حُرَّةً فَعِدَّتُهَا ثَلَاثَةُ قُرُوءٍ لِقَوْلِهِ تَعَالَى (وَالْمُطَلَّقَاتُ يَتَرَبَّصْنَ بِأَنْفُسِهِنَّ ثَلَاثَةَ قُرُوءٍ)

[142] al-Marghinani, *al-Hidayah*, 2:74:

"وإذا طلق الرجل امرأته طلاقا بائنا أو رجعيا أو وقعت الفرقة بينهما بغير طلاق وهي حرة ممن تحيض فعدتها ثلاثة أقراء" لقوله تعالى: {وَالْمُطَلَّقَاتُ يَتَرَبَّصْنَ بِأَنْفُسِهِنَّ ثَلَاثَةَ قُرُوءٍ} [البقرة: 228] والفرقة إذا كانت بغير طلاق فهي في معنى الطلاق لأن العدة وجبت للتعرف عن براءة الرحم في الفرقة الطارئة على النكاح وهذا يتحقق فيها والأقراء الحيض عندنا

3. **Four <u>lunar</u> months and ten days**: for a widowed woman that is not pregnant;

4. **Until she gives birth**: for a pregnant woman, regardless of whether the marriage ended by death of the husband or by pronouncement of divorce.[143]

5. **Illness**: 30 years for a woman who never experienced menstruation or 55 years for a woman who did experience menstruation but stopped due to reasons and complications.[144]

Note: even if it takes longer than usual (e.g. irregular menstrual cycles), the complete duration will have to be completed.[145]

<u>General related rulings</u>:

- *'Iddah* is an obligation on the woman (*fard*).

---

[143] See *al-Fatawa al-Hindiyyah*, 1:528: "...the *'iddah* of the pregnant woman is until she completes her pregnancy..."

وَعِدَّةُ الْحَامِلِ أَنْ تَضَعَ حَمْلَهَا

[144] However, the *fatwa* is given according to the Maliki position which is **1 year** *'iddah* due to the general hardship in following the strict Hanafi ruling. Ibn 'Abidin, *Radd al-Muhtar*, 3:509.

[145] *al-Fatawa al-Hindiyyah*, 1:195:

وَالْعِدَّةُ لِمَنْ لَمْ تَحِضْ لِصِغَرٍ أَوْ كِبَرٍ أَوْ بَلَغَتْ بِالسِّنِّ وَلَمْ تَحِضْ ثَلَاثَةَ أَشْهُرٍ كَذَا فِي النُّقَايَةِ وَكَذَا لَوْ رَأَتْ دَمَا يَوْمًا، ثُمَّ لَمْ تَرَ فَعِدَّتُهَا بِالشُّهُورِ هُوَ الصَّحِيحُ وَلَوْ رَأَتْ ثَلَاثَةَ دَمًا ، ثُمَّ انْقَطَعَ فَعِدَّتُهَا بِالْحَيْضِ، وَإِنْ طَالَ إِلَى أَنْ تَيْأَسَ كَذَا فِي الْعَتَّابِيَّةِ

- *'Iddah* is an obligation on the following women: (1) those from a legally correct (*sahih*) marriage; (2) those from a corrupt (*fasid*) marriage with consummation (and not mere seclusion).[146]
- *'Iddah* cannot be made up later if a person deliberately decides to avoid observing it. It is sinful to do that and requires serious repentance.
- *'Iddah* commences from the time the husband issues the divorce even if the woman did not know about it. However, if the *'iddah* period expired and then she learnt of the divorce given to her, then she does not have to endure the *'iddah* again.[147]
- *'Iddah* does not apply to a woman who is mature and has not consummated her marriage based on

---

[146] "...we can conclude that the difference between a corrupt (*fasid*) marriage and an invalid (*batil*) marriage is: That which there is a difference of opinion amongst the various Sunni *Mujtahid* Imams regarding its permissibility or otherwise such as marrying without witnesses, as Imam Malik (Allah have mercy on him) is of the opinion that having a specific number of witnesses is not a necessary condition (though it is necessary to publicize the marriage as much as possible), and also a contract where the corruptness is not in its essence". Mufti Ibn Adam, "Is waiting Period Obligatory on an Invalid Mut'a Marriage?" at http://islamqa.org/hanafi/daruliftaa/8394

[147] al-Haskafi, *Durr al-Mukhtar*, 3:520:

(ومبدأ العدة بعد الطلاق و) بعد (الموت) على الفور (وتنقضي العدة وإن جهلت) المرأة (بهما) أي بالطلاق والموت لأنها أجل فلا يشترط العلم بمضيه سواء اعترف بالطلاق، أو أنكر

al-Fatawa al-Hindiyya, 1:531:

ابتداء العدة في الطلاق عقيب الطلاق وفي الوفاة عقيب الوفاة فإن لم تعلم بالطلاق أو الوفاة حتى مضت مدة العدة فقد انقضت عدتها كذا في الهداية

Q.33:49. Hence, after divorce she can marry anyone she chooses.[148]

- The woman will spend her *'iddah* in her husband's home. He cannot force her out during this time.[149]
- *'Iddah* does not apply to a woman in the event of her committing adultery and fornication (*zina*).[150]
- Maintenance/expenses (see section on 'Nafaqah' above) are obligated on the husband during the *'iddah* period.[151]
- It is generally not permissible for a woman to leave the house during her *'iddah*.[152]
- It is generally not permissible for a woman to beautify, attract or adorn herself in the house during her *'iddah* (unless both seek reconciliation and return together as a couple).
- It is not permissible for a woman to seek another spouse during her *'iddah*.[153]

---

[148] *al-Fatawa al-Hindiyyah*, 1:552:

أربع من النساء لا عدة عليهن: المطلقة قبل الدخول

[149] al-Quduri, *al-Mukhtasar*, p.16.

و علي المعتدة أن تعتد في منزل الذي يضاف اليها بالسكني حال وقوع الفرقة

[150] *al-Fatawa al-Hindiyyah*, 1:526:

أربع من النساء لا عدة عليهن: المطلقة قبل الدخول

[151] Ibid., 1:552.
[152] al-Haskafi, *Durr al-Mukhtar*, 3:536:

(وتعتدان) أي معتدة طلاق وموت (في بيت وجبت فيه) ولا يخرجان منه

[153] al-Kasani, *al-Bada'i' al-Sana'i'*, 3:451:

- It is not permissible for a woman to marry another man during her 'iddah.[154]
- It is not permissible for a woman to disrespect her husband during her 'iddah.
- It is not permissible for a woman to mix with her husband during her 'iddah if he has given her talaq ba'in (irrevocable divorce).[155]
- It is not permissible for a woman to perform hajj – even with a mahram – during her 'iddah.
- It is not permissible for a woman to consider herself automatically in 'iddah if her husband is reported missing. The rules of the mafqud (absent) must be examined.
- It is permitted for a woman to work and earn a living during her 'iddah period if there is no family able to support her or if her ex-husband is deceased because

---

ومنها ألا تكون معتدة الغير...لأن بعض أحكام النكاح حالة العدة قائم فكان النكاح قائما من وجه والثابت من وجه كالثابت من كل وجه في باب المحرمات...سواء كانت العدة عن طلاق أو عن وفاة أو دخول في نكاح فاسد أو شبهة نكاح

[154] Ibid., 3:451.
[155] Ibn 'Abidin, Radd al-Muhtar, 3:537:

(ولا بد من سترة بينهما في البائن) لئلا يختلي بها بالأجنبية، ومفاده أن الحائل يمنع الخلوة المحرمة (وإن ضاق المنزل عليهما ، أو كان الزوج فاسقا فخروجه أولى) لأن مكثها واجب لا مكثه، ومفاده وجوب الحكم به ذكره الكمال (وحسن أن يجعل القاضي بينهما امرأة) ثقة .ترزق من بيت المال بحر عن تلخيص الجامع (قادرة على الحيلولة بينهما) وفي المجتبى الأفضل الحيلولة بستر، ولو فاسقا فبامرأة...قال ابن عابدين: (قوله : ومفاده) أي مفاد التعليل بوجوب مكثها وجوب الحكم به أي بخروجه عنها .وقولهم : وخروجه أولى لعل المراد أنه أرجح، كما يقال : إذا تعارض محرم ومبيح فالمحرم أولى، أو أرجح فإنه يراد الوجوب فتح . قوله : وفي المجتبى إلخ) حيث قال : والأفضل أن يحال بينهما في البيتوتة بستر إلا أن يكون فاسقا فيحال بامرأة ثقة، وإن تعذر فلتخرج هي وخروجه أولى ا هـ ملخصا، وفيه مخالفة لما مر، فإن السترة لا بد منها كما عبر المصنف تبعا للهداية، وهو الظاهر لحرمة الخلوة بالأجنبية

it is a necessity that she earn to feed herself and children (if any).[156]

- It is permitted for a woman to return to her husband if he shows indications of that (e.g. telling her, cohabiting with her, kissing her, etc.) by revoking his divorce during her *'iddah*.

- It is permitted for a woman to complete her *'iddah* in another place other than her marital home for fear of safety or *fitnah*, e.g. assault, abuse, etc.

- It is permitted for the woman to complete her *'iddah* in the place where she was issued her *talaq*.

§2. Halalah

If a husband issued three *talaqs*, he has irretrievably ended his marriage with his wife. She is no longer lawful for him. Both must separate and the woman must enter into her *'iddah* and observe it correctly. The only conceivable way he can return to a lawful relationship with his ex-wife is if a process called "*halalah*" (lit. 'lawful')[157] took place:[158]

---

[156] Ibid., 5:224-225:

بيان للفرق بين معتدة الموت ومعتدة الطلاق قال في الهداية : وأما المتوفى عنها زوجها فلأنه لا نفقة لها فتحتاج إلى الخروج نهارا لطلب المعاش وقد يمتد إلى أن يهجم الليل ولا كذلك المطلقة لأن النفقة دارة عليها من مال زوجها ا هـ قال في الفتح : والحاصل أن مدار حل خروجها بسبب قيام شغل المعيشة فيتقدر بقدره ، فمتى انقضت حاجتها لا يحل لها بعد ذلك صرف الزمان خارج بيتها

[157] http://en.wikipedia.org/wiki/Nikah_Halala
[158] See al-Marghinani, *al-Hidayah*, p.379:

وإن كان الطلاق ثلاثا في الحرة أو ثنتين في الأمة لم تحل له حتى تنكح زوجا غيره نكاحا صحيحا ويدخل بها ثم يطلقها أو يموت عنها والأصل فيه قوله تعالى { فإن طلقها فلا تحل له من بعد حتى تنكح زوجا غيره }... والشرط الإيلاج دون الإنزال لأنه كمال ومبالغة فيه والكمال قيد زائد

Halalah is when the divorcee spends her *iddat* of divorce after which she marries another person. The new marriage is then consummated. The second husband then divorces his wife or passes away. The woman then waits for her *iddat* to finish after which she may re-marry the first husband if she wishes to. This procedure should be coincidental, not planned. For example, a husband and wife split up and they wish to reconcile but they cannot because an irrevocable *talaaq* has been issued. Upon learning about this, a third person decides to help reconcile the marriage. So he marries the divorcee, consummates the relationship and divorces her. All this happens without him divulging his intention to anyone else. This will be permissible.[159] However, for the parties to plan such a procedure is impermissible. Rasulullah *sallallahu alaihi wasallam* has said:

عَنْ أَبِي هُرَيْرَةَ، رَضِيَ اللَّهُ عَنْهُ قَالَ: قَالَ رَسُولُ اللَّهِ صَلَّى اللهُ عَلَيْهِ وَسَلَّمَ: لَعَنْ اللَّهُ الْمُحَلِّلَ وَالْمُحَلَّلَ لَهُ

"May Allah curse the one who does *halalah* and the one for whom it is done."[160]

- In other words, for a man to remarry his ex-wife, she would have had to be lawfully married to another man, consummated that marriage and then divorced

---

[159] Mawlana S. Ibn Muhammad, "Permissibility of Halalah" at http://askimam.org/public/question_detail/19858
[160] See al-Bayhaqi, *al-Sunan al-Kubra*, 7:339.

lawfully to then be free to marry her ex-husband (or any other person).

Some conditions:

1. A legal marriage has to take place (i.e. offer and acceptance, etc.).[161]
2. Penetration has to take place in the marriage; it is not enough to merely marry (excludes mere seclusion or anal penetration).[162]
3. Husband being alive (if he is not then she will have to marry again).[163]
4. No verbal intention or explicit mention of *halalah* being the reason for the marriage (according to Abu Yusuf).[164]

- One of the wisdoms behind the *halalah* process is to prevent the husband from divorcing and re-marrying his wife at a whim, i.e. to prevent abuse from the husband into trapping her in a marriage or seemingly owning her.

- *Halalah* however is **not** a Shariah method for an ex-husband to get back with his ex-wife:

  Many people with regards to this are mistaken. The general misconception is that marrying another man (*Halala*) is a solution provided by Shariah in order for the husband and wife to get back together. This is, however, not the case. The meaning of *Halala* is that, if the woman after being divorced and after

---

[161] Mufti Abdul Jaleel Qasmi, *The Complete System of Divorce*, pp.53-54.
[162] Ibid., pp.55 and 67.
[163] Ibid., pp.60-61.
[164] Ibid., pp.61-63.

observing her waiting period wished to marry another man, she can do so. This second husband by total coincidence and on his own accord also divorced her after having sexual intercourse with her, then after observing the full waiting period, she can remarry her first husband. It should be remembered that, this is not a solution provided by Shariah. Once three divorces are pronounced, the marriage is over and there is no getting together again. But if by coincidence, she married another man and he to by coincidence (after having sexual intercourse with her) divorced her, then she, after the *Iddah* is over, can remarry her first husband. If *Nikah* was performed on the condition of *Halala* or by fixing a fee to be paid to the second man, then this is a grave sin and unlawful. The Prophet (Allah bless him and give him peace) said: "Allah's curse is on the one who makes a contract or agreement for *Halala* (Both the one who carries out *Halala* and the one who it is done for." (*Sunan* al Darami / *Mishkat al Masabih*) However, if there is only an intention of *Halala* in the heart and no verbal agreement was made, then according to the majority of *Fuqaha*, this is permissible and valid (*Radd al-Muhtar*).[165]

Some related rulings:

- If a man marries a woman to deliberately divorce her in order to enable her to get back with her ex-husband, the act will stand having legally occurred but the individuals are sinful for doing it.[166]

---

[165] Mufti Ibn Adam, "Divorce, Waiting Period (idda) and Marrying Another Man (halala)" at http://islamqa.org/hanafi/daruliftaa/7807
[166] Ibn 'Abidin, *Radd al-Muhtar*, 3:414:

- "The person performing the second marriage will be rewarded if he marries with the sole intention of reconciling the wife to her former husband. The curse in the *Hadith* is when *Halaalah* is done with remuneration".[167]

§3. Types of Talaq

In Islamic Law as understood by Hanafi jurists, there are three types of divorce each with their descriptions:[168]

(وكره) التزوج للثاني (تحريما) لحديث { لعن المحلل والمحلل له } (بشرط التحليل) كتزوجتك على أن أحللك (وإن حلت للأول) لصحة النكاح وبطلان الشرط فلا يجبر على الطلاق كما حققه الكمال، خلافا لما زعمه البزازي : (أما إذا أضمر ذلك لا) يكره (وكان (الرجل) مأجورا) لقصد الإصلاح، وتأويل اللعن إذا شرط الأجر ذكره البزازي...قال ابن عابدين: (قوله : وكره التزوج للثاني) كذا في البحر : لكن في القهستاني : وكره للأول والثاني ، وعزاه محشي مسكين إلى الحموي عن الظهيرية ، وينبغي أن يزاد المرأة بل هي أولى من الأول في الكراهة بشرط التحليل لأن العقد بشرط التحليل إنما جرى بينها وبين الثاني، والأول ساع في ذلك ومتسبب والمباشر أولى من المتسبب ولفظ الحديث يشمل الكل، فإن المحلل له يصدق على المرأة أيضا (قوله : لحديث { لعن المحلل والمحلل له }) بإضافة " حديث " إلى " لعن "، فهو حكاية للمعنى، وإلا فلفظ الحديث كما في الفتح " { لعن الله المحلل والمحلل له } " وهو كذلك في بعض النسخ (قوله : بشرط التحليل) تأويل للحديث بحمل اللعن على ذلك، ويأتي تمام الكلام عليه (قوله : وإن حلت للأول إلخ) هذا قول الإمام

[167] Mufti Ebrahim Desai, "Can Halala take place only by Arrangement?" at http://islamqa.org/hanafi/askimam/15941
[168] See al-Zuhayli, *al-Fiqh al-Islami wa Adillatuhu*, 9:6948-6950:

فذهب الحنفية إلى أن التقسيم ثلاثي، أي أن الطلاق ثلاثة أنواع: أحسن الطلاق، والطلاق الحسن، والطلاق البدعي:

أحسن الطلاق: أن يطلق الرجل امرأته تطليقة واحدة، في طهر لم يجامعها فيه، ويتركها حتى تنقضي عدتها؛ لأن الصحابة رضي الله عنهم كانوا يستحبون ألا يزيد الطلاق على واحدة حتى تنقضي العدة، فإن هذا أفضل عندهم من أن يطلقها الرجل ثلاثاً عند كل طهر واحدة، ولأنه أبعد من الندامة، لتمكنه من التدارك، وأقل ضرراً بالمرأة.

1. **Talaq Ahsan** (أحسن الطلاق): This is when only one divorce is issued to a woman who is in a state of purity prior to any consummation of the marriage where after she observes her *'iddah* without any hindrance or problem as a consequence of which she is a free woman to marry anyone she chooses.

2. **Talaq al-Hasan** (الطلاق الحسن): this is also known as the 'Sunnah way of divorce' (طلاق السنة) which refers to the husband's pronouncements of divorce three times but in three separate states of the woman's purity, i.e. she receives three *talaqs* in three different periods when she is pure.

3. **Talaq al-Bid'ah** (طلاق البدعة): this is when a husband issues a divorce contrary to the Qur'anic injunction and Prophetic way that also brings hardship on the woman. It stands legally effective even though it is

---

والطلاق الحسن: هو طلاق السنة: وهوأن يطلق المدخول بها ثلاثاً في ثلاثة أطهار، في كل طهر تطليقة، يستقبل الطهر استقبالاً، عملاً بأمره صلَّى الله عليه وسلم في حديث ابن عمر المتقدم.

وطلاق البدعة: أن يطلقها ثلاثاً أوائنتين بكلمة واحدة، أو يطلقها ثلاثاً في طهر واحد؛ لأن الأصل في الطلاق الحظر، لما فيه من قطع الزواج الذي تعلقت به المصالح الدينية والدنيوية، والإباحة إنما هي للحاجة إلى الخلاص، ولا حاجة إلى الجمع في الثلاث، أو في طهر واحد؛ لأن الحاجة تندفع بالواحدة، وتمام الخلاص في المفرق على الأطهار، والزيادة إسراف، فكان بدعة. فإذا فعل ذلك وقع الطلاق، وبانت المرأة منه، وكان آثماً عاصياً، والطلاق مكروه تحريماً؛ لأن الحظر أو النهي لمعنى في غير الطلاق وهو فوات مصالح الدين والدنيا، مثل البيع وقت النداء لصلاة الجمعة صحيح مكروه لمعنى في غيره، والصلاة في الأرض المغصوبة صحيحة مكروهة لمعنى في غيرها، وكذا إيقاع أكثر من طلقة، إذ لا حاجة إليه. لذا تجب رجعة المطلقة في الحيض أو النفاس، على الأصح رفعاً للمعصية وللأمر السابق: «مره فليراجعها» فإذا طهرت طلقها إن شاء، أوأمسكها.

unlawful to issue it in that manner.[169] There are three major sinful types of *talaq*:

[a] To issue a *talaq* when the woman is in her menstrual period is contrary to Prophetic practice. This is a sinful method of *talaq* and the Prophetic *hadith* is clear on this. The husband will have to take back the wife and wait until she attains purity.[170]

[b] To issue *talaq* to his wife immediately after having sexual intercourse with her because: it may be at a time when she is actually pregnant (but does not know it) and a *talaq* will put her into the *'iddah* and the duration of the *'iddah* for a pregnant woman is the duration of the entire pregnancy. This is a difficult duration.

[c] To issue three *talaqs* simultaneously, i.e. at one time. This permanently ends the marriage and no immediate remarriage is lawful.

---

[169] al-Kasani, *al-Bada'i' al-Sana'i'*, 3:96:

وأما حكم طلاق البدعة فهو أنه واقع عند عامة العلماء

[170] See al-Nasa'i, *Sunan* (#3398):

أنه طلق امرأته وهي حائض فردها عليه رسول الله صلى الله عليه وسلم حتى طلقها وهي طاهر

Ibn 'Abidin, *Radd al-Muhtar*, 3:246:

(وتجب رجعتها) - أي المطلقة في الحيض - على الصحيح - (فيه) أي الحيض رفعا للمعصية ، فإذا طهرت طلقها إن شاء أو أمسكها

§4. Categories of Talaq

The categories of divorce are broadly two: [1] *Talaq* and [2] *Khul'*. Each type will be outlined below in a little more detail. The laws pertaining to divorce are intricate and detailed and hence require careful study as well as further research and engagement.

صريح: **Clear Divorce** (*sarih*) → رجعي: **Revocable** (*raj'i*)

كناية: **Unclear Divorce** (*kinayah*) → بائنة: **Irrevocable** (*ba'inah*)

1.

Clear Revocable Divorce (طلاق رجعي صريح): It is called 'clear' because the pronouncement of *talaq* is effective through explicit and unambiguous words and it is 'revocable' because the husband can take back the wife during her *'iddah* period without needing to renew the *nikah* contract.

Related rulings:

1. Intention (*niyyah*) is not a requirement because the clear words that are uttered are given consideration over an inner intention.[171]

---

[171] al-Mawsili, *al-Ikhtiyar, li-Ta'lil al-Mukhtar*, 3:167:

(وصريح الطلاق لا يحتاج إلى نية) لأنه موضوع له شرعا فكان حقيقة، والحقيقة لا تحتاج إلى نية، ويعقب الرجعة لقوله تعالى { وبعولتهن أحق بردهن} ولو نوى الإبانة فهو رجعي لأنه نوى ما ضد ما وضع له شرعا.

2. A revocable divorce (*raj'i*) takes effect (where as explained 'revocable' means the option is open for the husband to reconcile with the wife without renewing the *nikah* bond).[172]

3. A revocable divorce puts a woman into her *'iddah* of three menstrual cycles (see the section on Waiting Period').[173]

4. If a husband does not take back his wife during the *'iddah* of one revocable divorce, then she is freed from the bond of *nikah* (marriage) and he has no rights over her. If the husband desires to reconcile with his wife thereafter, then he must undergo a new *nikah* procedure, i.e. remarry her.[174]

Words that indicate a clear *talaq*:

*   Words/phrases that contain <*talaq*> or <divorce> or its import in any language.[175]
*   Words/phrases that explicitly indicate severing the marital bond or its import in any language.[176]

Examples:

1. 'Divorcee!'
2. 'You're divorced!'
3. 'I divorce you!'
4. 'You are no longer my wife!'

---

[172] Ibn 'Abidin, *Radd al-Muhtar*, 2:219 and 592.
[173] Ibid., 2:219.
[174] Ibid., 2:646.
[175] Ibid., 2:590.
[176] Ibid., 2:590f.

5. 'Between you and me is a divorce!'[177]

Other expressions include:

6. 'I have let you go!'
7. 'I have freed you!'
8. 'You are *haram* for me!'[178]

2.

Unclear irrevocable Divorce (طلاق بائن كناية): It is called 'unclear' because the pronouncement of *talaq* is effective through ambiguous words and it is 'irrevocable' because the husband cannot take back the wife during her *'iddah* unless he renews the *nikah* contract.[179]

---

[177] See *al-Fatawa al-Hindiyyah*, 1:354.

[178] See *al-Fatawa al-Bazzaziyyah*, 1:188 and 199.

[179] al-Kasani, *al-Bada'i' al-Sana'i'*, 3:105-106:

أَمَّا النَّوْعُ الْأَوَّلُ فَهُوَ كُلُّ لَفْظٍ يُسْتَعْمَلُ فِي الطَّلَاقِ وَيُسْتَعْمَلُ فِي غَيْرِهِ نَحْوُ قَوْلِهِ: أَنْتِ بَائِنٌ، أَنْتِ عَلَيَّ حَرَامٌ خَلِيَّةٌ بَرِيَّةٌ بَتَّةً أَمْرُكِ بِيَدِكِ اخْتَارِي اعْتَدِّي اسْتَبْرِئِي رَحِمَك أَنْتِ وَاحِدَةً خَلَّيْتُ سَبِيلَكِ سَرَّحْتُكِ حَبْلُكِ عَلَى غَارِبِكِ فَارَقْتُكِ خَالَعْتُكِ – وَلَمْ يَذْكُرْ الْعِوَضَ – لَا سَبِيلَ لِي عَلَيْكِ لَا مِلْكَ لِي عَلَيْكِ لَا نِكَاحَ لِي عَلَيْكِ أَنْتِ حُرَّةٌ قُومِي اُخْرُجِي اُغْرُبِي انْطَلِقِي تَقَنَّعِي اسْتَتِرِي تَزَوَّجِي ابْتَغِي الْأَزْوَاجَ الْحَقِي بِأَهْلِكِ وَنَحْوُ ذَلِكَ. سُمِّيَ هَذَا النَّوْعُ مِنْ الْأَلْفَاظِ كِنَايَةً، لِأَنَّ الْكِنَايَةَ فِي اللُّغَةِ اسْمٌ لَفْظٍ اسْتَتَرَ الْمُرَادُ مِنْهُ عِنْدَ السَّامِعِ

وَإِذَا احْتَمَلَتْ هَذِهِ الْأَلْفَاظُ الطَّلَاقَ وَغَيْرَ الطَّلَاقِ فَقَدْ اسْتَتَرَ الْمُرَادُ مِنْهَا عِنْدَ السَّامِعِ، فَافْتَقَرَتْ إلَى النِّيَّةِ لِتَعْيِينِ الْمُرَادِ وَلَا خِلَافَ فِي هَذِهِ الْجُمْلَةِ إلَّا فِي ثَلَاثَةِ أَلْفَاظٍ وَهِيَ قَوْلُهُ: سَرَّحْتُكِ، وَفَارَقْتُكِ، وَأَنْتِ وَاحِدَةٌ فَقَالَ أَصْحَابُنَا: قَوْلُهُ: سَرَّحْتُكِ وَفَارَقْتُكِ مِنْ الْكِنَايَاتِ لَا يَقَعُ الطَّلَاقُ بِهِمَا إلَّا بِقَرِينَةِ النِّيَّةِ كَسَائِرِ الْكِنَايَاتِ وَإِذَا احْتَمَلَتْ هَذِهِ الْأَلْفَاظُ الطَّلَاقَ وَغَيْرَ الطَّلَاقِ فَقَدْ اسْتَتَرَ الْمُرَادُ مِنْهَا عِنْدَ السَّامِعِ، فَافْتَقَرَتْ إلَى النِّيَّةِ لِتَعْيِينِ الْمُرَادِ وَلَا خِلَافَ فِي هَذِهِ الْجُمْلَةِ إلَّا فِي ثَلَاثَةِ أَلْفَاظٍ وَهِيَ قَوْلُهُ: سَرَّحْتُكِ، وَفَارَقْتُكِ، وَأَنْتِ وَاحِدَةٌ فَقَالَ أَصْحَابُنَا: قَوْلُهُ: سَرَّحْتُكِ وَفَارَقْتُكِ مِنْ الْكِنَايَاتِ لَا يَقَعُ الطَّلَاقُ بِهِمَا إلَّا بِقَرِينَةِ النِّيَّةِ كَسَائِرِ الْكِنَايَاتِ

Related rulings:

1. Intention (*niyyah*) is a requirement because unclear words that are uttered do not automatically generate a divorce due to their ambiguity. Thus, the husband's intention must be ascertained. If he intended *talaq*, then one *talaq* will fall, if he intended, two the two will fall, etc.

2. Ascertaining the circumstantial indications (*dalalat al-hal*) will be required (details given below).

3. An irrevocable divorce (*ba'in*) takes effect (where as explained 'irrevocable' means the option is not open for the husband to reconcile with the wife without renewing the *nikah* bond).

4. An irrevocable divorce puts a woman into her '*iddah* of three menstrual cycles.

Words that indicate an unclear *talaq*:

- Words/phrases that do not contain the word <*talaq*> or <divorce> or its import in any language.[180]
- Words/phrases that <u>do not</u> explicitly indicate severing the marital bond or its import in any language but require an interpretation due to its ambiguity.[181]

[180] Ibn Nujaym, *al-Bahr al-Ra'iq*, 3:298.
[181] Ibid., 3:298-300.

Examples:

1. 'You're separated!'
2. 'Lonely woman!'
3. 'Isolated woman!'
4. '*Batta*!'
5. 'Start counting your '*iddah* days!'
6. 'Free your womb!'
7. 'You're single!'
8. 'I've opened your way for you!'
9. 'I have untied the knot!'
10. 'I have dismissed you!'
11. 'I have no control over you!'
12. 'I have no *nikah* with you!'
13. 'Get out!'
14. 'Get lost!'
15. 'Leave home!'
16. 'Find another home!'
17. 'Go to your family!'
18. 'I have gifted you to your family!'
19. 'You're a free woman!'
20. 'The matter is in your hands!'[182]

Other expressions include:

21. 'Move out!'
22. 'It's over!'
23. 'We have no future!'
24. 'Pack your bags!'
25. 'We're finished!'

---

[182] See al-Mawsili, *al-Ikhtiyar li-Ta'lil al-Mukhtar*, 3:176:

وألفاظ البائن قوله : أنت بائن، بتة، بتلة، حرام، حبلك على غاربك، خلية، برية، الحقي بأهلك، وهبتك لأهلك، سرحتك، فارقتك، أمرك بيدك، تقنعي، استبري، أنت حرة، اغربي، اخرجي، ابتغي الأزواج

26. 'Find someone else!'
27. 'Leave home!'

§5. Circumstantial Indications

Often, ambiguous words may be removed through analysis or investigation of the circumstances (*hal*) in which those words were uttered in addition to the intention.[183] In other words, the context of these utterances helps eliminate the doubtful elements regarding whether a *talaq* was intended or not. It happens that a husband actually intended divorce but couched it behind certain ambiguous expressions. Given the circumstances he was in at the time and through removing the means of doubt, the ruling could very well be affected by these circumstances coming to light. The books of *fiqh* outline three circumstances that are relevant regarding unclear and ambiguous (*kinayah*) words and they are given in the table below:

Circumstance 1	Circumstance 2	Circumstance 3
Normal state	*State of anger*	*State of discussion*
This is when the husband is in a normal and relaxed state; if he utters an	This is when the husband utters unclear or ambiguous (*kinayah*)	This is when the husband and wife are discussing the subject of *talaq* and the husband

---

[183] Ibid., 3:176f:

(وكنايات الطلاق لا يقع بها إلا بنية أو بدلالة الحال) لاحتمالها الطلاق وغيره لأنها غير موضوعة له فلا يتعين إلا بالتعيين، وهو أن ينويه أو تدل عليه الحال فتترجح إرادته

ambiguous (*kinayah*) word/expression in this state then unless his intention for *talaq* is proved, no *talaq* will be effective by mere utterance of such words.[184]

words/expression in a state of anger because of a heated argument or an altercation. Intention will need to be proved otherwise no *talaq* will be effective by mere utterance of the words.[185]

utters an ambiguous (*kinayah*) word/expression in this state then unless his intention for *talaq* is proved, no *talaq* will be effective by mere utterance of such words.[186]

Given each circumstance, additional aspects will have to be considered and assessed beyond the intention and utterance in order to determine whether a *talaq* occurred in that instance or not such as:

1. Specific actions.
2. Character of the husband.
3. History of the relationship.
4. Previous behaviour,
5. etc.

Related rulings:

- *Talaq* is not language specific.
- If one *talaq ba'in* occurs, then even if a man utters more pronouncements of divorce, it will not be effective.

---

[184] Ibn 'Abidin, *Radd al-Muhtar*, 2:640.
[185] Ibid., 2:640-641.
[186] Ibid., 2:640-641.

§6. Delegating Talaq (*tafwid*)

The Shariah permits the right to conduct positive *talaq* to the wife. This designation of right is known as *talaq al-tafwid* ('delegated divorce'). This right enables the wife to pronounce or effect a *talaq* just like the husband. The condition of this mode of *talaq* is: [1] the woman must initiate the proposal of the *talaq* to the husband and not vice versa. This must be stipulated as a condition before or during the *nikah* contract is concluded.

Delegated divorce as explained in the books of *fiqh* is delivered through three modes and they are:[187]

Delegation (*tafwid*)	Representation (*tawkil*)	Letter (*risalah*)
This is where a husband directly grants permission for the wife the right to self-divorce, i.e. he directly devolves	This is where a husband appoints a legal agent or representative on his behalf to delegate the right of divorce to the wife.	This is where the husband issues a written permission to delegate the right of divorce to the wife.

---

[187] al-Haskafi, *Durr al-Mukhtar*, 3:314-316:

باب تفويض الطلاق لما ذكر ما يوقعه بنفسه بنوعيه ذكر ما يوقعه غيره بإذنه . وأنواعه ثلاثة تفويض، وتوكيل، ورسالة وألفاظ التفويض ثلاثة : تخيير وأمر بيد، ومشيئة (قال لها اختاري أو أمرك بيدك ينوي) تفويض (الطلاق) لأنها كناية فلا يعملان بلا نية (أو طلقي نفسك فلها أن تطلق في مجلس علمها به) مشافهة أو إخبارا (وإن طال) يوما أو أكثر ما لم يوقته ويمضي الوقت قبل علمها (ما لم تقم) لتبدل مجلسها حقيقة (أو) حكما بأن (تعمل ما يقطعه) مما يدل على الإعراض لأنه تمليك فيتوقف على قبول في المجلس لا توكيل، فلم يصح رجوعه، حتى لو خيرها ثم حلف أن لا يطلقها فطلقت لم يحنث في الأصح (لا) تطلق (بعده) أي المجلس (إلا إذا زاد) في قوله طلقي نفسك وأخواته (متى شئت أو متى ما شئت أو إذا شئت أو إذا ما شئت) فلا يتقيد بالمجلس (ولم يصح رجوعه) لما مر.

the right to her.

Related rulings:

- The woman must be well aware she has been given this right of *talaq*.[188]
- Acceptance of this right of delegated divorce must be concluded and accepted in the same sitting (*majlis*) that she was made aware of.[189]
- A man does not have the right to revoke his permission to grant his wife divorce after having delegated it except in certain instances such as the woman revoking her proposal for a delegated divorce, or if she leaves the gathering or declines altogether.[190]
- If the husband specifies a time period for when she obtains the permission to a delegated divorce, then until that time arrives she cannot exercise her right.[191]
- If the husband specifies only permission of one *talaq* for the wife, then she may only exercise that one permission of *talaq* and no more.[192]
- The language of *tafwid* ('delegation') must be clear in transferring the meaning of *talaq*, e.g. 'I give you the right of divorce', 'you can choose to divorce yourself', 'the matter is in your hands', 'you have the choice', etc.[193]

---

[188] Mufti Abdul Jaleel Qasmi, *The Complete System of Divorce*, p.168.
[189] Ibid., pp.168-169.
[190] Ibid., pp.183-186.
[191] Ibid., p.170.
[192] Ibid., p.170.
[193] Ibid., pp.171-176.

- The moment a wife obtains the permission to divorce herself through a delegated divorce, then any words that cause divorce if done by the husband also holds for the wife.[194]

§7. Khul'

The *khula'* is a method open to women for effecting a divorce – thus it is a female initiated divorce. This is the case where a woman acquires an exit from her marriage by returning her dowry (*mahr*) or some monetary compensation. The word "*khul'*" (خلع) linguistically means 'to separate', 'to remove' and 'to pull away'.[195] In legal terms, it is the wife's filing for exit from her marriage bond based on legal grounds that result in a *talaq ba'in*:[196]

---

[194] Ibid., p.175.

[195] Lane, *Arabic-English* Lexicon, Book 1, p.790. See also http://en.wikipedia.org/wiki/Khula and Mufti Ibn Adam who states:

> *Khul'* is an Arabic term that literally means 'to take out' and 'remove'. The Arabs say: "*Khala'tu al-libas*" (I took off my cloths). Similarly, Allah Almighty said to Sayyiduna Musa (Peace be upon him) when he went to receive the sacred law: **"Verily I am your lord! Therefore, put off (*fakhla'*) your shoes"** (Surah Ta Ha, 12). The lexical definition of *Khul'* as explained by the famous Hanafi *Mujtahid*, Ibn Humam is as Follows: "To remove the union of marriage in exchange of a financial settlement with the words of *Khul'*" (Ibn Humam, *Fath al-Qadir*, 3/1999). Similar to other agreements and transactions, an agreement on *Khul'* will also come into effect by acceptance and offer (al-Kasani, *Bada'i al-Sana'i*, 3/145 & *Radd al-Muhtar*, 2/606). See "Questions about Separation" at http://spa.qibla.com

[196] Ibn Nujaym, *al-Bahr al-Ra'iq*, 4:70-71:

In the situation where a woman can no longer remain in the marriage of her husband and all attempts to save the marriage have failed, then the ideal solution would be for the wife to obtain a divorce from the husband. The husband, seeing that the marriage is futile and there is no hope of reconcilement, should also issue one divorce according to the prescribed method in Shariah.

باب الخلع لما اشترك مع الإيلاء في أن كلا منهما قد يكون معصية وقد يكون مباحا وزاد الخلع عليه بتسمية المال أخر عنه لأنه بمنزلة المركب من المفرد وقدما على الظهار واللعان لأنهما لا ينفكان عن المعصية وهو لغة النزع يقال خلعت النعل وغيره خلعا نزعته وخالعت المرأة زوجها مخالعة إذا افتدت منه وطلقها على الفدية فخلعها هو خلعا والاسم الخلع بالضم وهو استعارة من خلع اللباس لأن كل واحد منهما لباس للآخر فإذا فعلا ذلك فكان كل واحد نزع لباسه عنه كذا في المصباح

(قوله الواقع به، وبالطلاق على مال طلاق بائن) أي بالخلع الشرعي أما الخلع فقوله عليه الصلاة والسلام الخلع تطليقة بائنة، ولأنه يحتمل الطلاق حتى صار من الكنايات، والواقع بالكناية بائن

al-Zayla'i, *Tabyin al-Haqa'iq*, 3:182: "and its ruling results in a *talaq ba'in*..."

وحكمه وقوع الطلاق البائن

al-Haskafi, *Durr al-Mukhtar*, 3:440:

لو قال : خلعتك – ناويا الطلاق – فإنه يقع بائنا غير مسقط للحقوق لعدم توقفه عليها

al-Sarakhsi, *al-Mabsut*, 3:141:

والخلع تطليقة بائنة عندنا

Ibn al-Humam, *Fath al-Qadir*, 4:58:

قوله فإذا فعلا ذلك وقع بالخلع تطليقة بائنة ولزمها المال (هذا حكم الخلع عند جماهير الأئمة من السلف والخلف

However, in the case where the husband refuses to issue a divorce, the wife may persuade the husband to enter into an agreement of *Khul'* (a release for payment from the wife). The wife may also opt to forgive the husband from paying her dowry (*mahr*).[197]

The only difference between divorce and *khul'* is that a divorce is given by the man without demanding a financial payment form [*sic.*] the wife, whereas in *khul'*, the wife receives the divorce in return for a financial payment. This is usually in a situation where the husband in unwilling to give the divorce and the wife persuades him to issue the divorce in return of this payment.[198]

If there is no compatibility between the spouses and the husband is not willing to issue a divorce then it will be permissible for the spouses to do *Khula'*. *Khula'* is when the couple relinquish their rights of marriage using the word *khula'* or any other word which holds the same implications. For example the wife forgoes her right of *mahr* and the husband forgoes his possession of *nikāh*, or the wife gives some money and the husband leaves his right of *nikāh*. *Khula'* takes the ruling of an irrevocable divorce *(talāq bāin)*. *Khula'* will be completed one [*sic.*] the couple completes *ījāb* (proposal) and *qabūl* (acceptance).[199]

---

[197] See Mufti Ibn Adam, "Questions about Separation" at http://spa.qibla.com
[198] See Mufti Ibn Adam, "Difference Between Khula and Divorce" at http://spa.qibla.com
[199] See Mufti I. E. Moosa, "If a Couple agrees to Khula" at http://askimam.org/public/question_detail/19363

General rulings:

1. **The consent of the husband**: *khul'* has to be activated by the consent of the husband who cannot be forced to permit it. Therefore a woman must make a plea, request or petition for the divorce.[200]

2. **Words denoting *khul'***: any clause or words identical to or denoting the meaning of *"khul'"* must be clearly stated. Any terms that also are in the language of a general commercial transaction will also be valid.[201]

3. **Valid legal grounds**: it is sinful for a woman to seek *khul'* without valid Shariah grounds due to the strong words of the Messenger of Allah.[202]

---

[200] On this there is juristic consensus. See *Kitab al-Umm* of Imam al-Shafi'i:

ولا يجبر الزوجان على توكيلهما إن لم يوكلا

[201] See *al-Fatawa al-Hindiyyah*, 1:488: "And the meaning of *khul'* is removing the union of *nikah* with something in exchange with the wording of *khul'* as mentioned in *Fath al-Qadir*."

الخلع إزالة ملك النكاح ببدل بلفظ الخلع كذا في فتح القدير وقد يصح بلفظ البيع والشراء وقد يكون بالفارسية كذا في الظهيرية وشرطه شرط الطلاق وحكمه وقوع الطلاق البائن كذا في التبيين

[202] The Prophet said: **"Any woman who seeks divorce unnecessarily then even the scent of paradise is unlawful for her"**. al-Tirmidhi, *Sunan*, 3:485:

أَيُّمَا امْرَأَةٍ سَأَلَتْ زَوْجَهَا طَلَاقًا فِي غَيْرِ مَا بَأْسٍ فَحَرَامٌ عَلَيْهَا رَائِحَةُ الْجَنَّةِ

4. **Offer and acceptance:** The *khula'* is concluded with offer and acceptance, i.e. a mutual agreement of separation because an exchange is taking place (a woman offering something in exchange for her release form the marital bond).[203]

5. **Woman's right:** The *khul'* is a right given by the Shariah to the woman – it cannot be prevented or taken away by anyone.

6. **Out of Court:** A court does not have the right to impose a decree of *khul'* on behalf of the husband. His consent is required. Only in the case of unlawful impediment by the husband can the wife seek annulment through a court, Shariah body or council of scholars.

7. **Khalifah's authority:** the khalifah/Sultan has the authority to effect *khul'*.[204]

---

[203] al-Bukhari, *al-Muhit al-Burhani*, 5:59:

ومن جانب المرأة يعتبر بالإيجاب والقبول كما في باب البيع

al-Fatawa al-Tatarkhaniyyah, 3:453:

في الملخص والايضاح: الخلع عقد يفتقر الى الايجاب والقبول يثبت الفرقة ويستحق عليها العوض. وفي السغناقي هو عبارة عن اخذ مال المراة بازاء ملك النكاح بلفظ الخلع

[204] al-Sarakhsi, *al-Mabsut*, 6:1:173: "And the *khul'* divorce is permitted with the sultan and any other person because it is an act based on mutual consent..."

والخلع جائز عند السلطان وغيره لأنه عقد يعتمد التراضي

Ibn Hazm, *al-Mahalla*, 9:248:

8. **Dowry and *khul'***: If a husband has been oppressive and unjust in the marriage and wife seeks *khul'*, he should not demand the *mahr* back nor any monetary compensation.

Related rulings:

1. If *khul'* is enacted through coercion, then it stands as effective.
2. If *khul'* is enacted through a 'deed' (document) or writing then it is valid.
3. If *khul'* is enacted, then the woman enters her *'iddah* (see §. 'waiting period' in the handout for the rulings related to that).

ليس في الآية، ولا في شيء من السنن أن للحكمين أن يفرقا، ولا أن ذلك للحاكم

Chapter 8: "Marriage and Divorce: *Tackling Common Scenarios*"

———— Ψ ————

§1. Preliminaries

- When an irrevocable *talaq* takes place (i.e. the marriage completely dissolves), the following consequences arises:

Effects of a *talaq* scenario:

1. The woman is no longer the legal wife of the husband.
2. Marriage breakdown.
3. Woman enters her 'waiting period' ('*iddah*) which is endured as follows:

[a] If she experiences menses, her '*iddah* will be three menses (menstrual cycles).[205]

[b] If she does not experience menses, her '*iddah* will be three months.[206]

---

[205] al-Marghinani, *al-Hidayah*, 2:274:

وإذا طلق الرجل امرأته طلاقا بائنا أو رجعيا أو وقعت الفرقة بينهما بغير طلاق وهي حرة ممن تحيض فعدتها ثلاثة أقراء لقوله تعالى: {وَالْمُطَلَّقَاتُ يَتَرَبَّصْنَ بِأَنْفُسِهِنَّ ثَلاثَةَ قُرُوءٍ} [البقرة: 228] والفرقة إذا كانت بغير طلاق فهي في معنى الطلاق لأن العدة وجبت للتعرف عن براءة الرحم في الفرقة الطارئة على النكاح وهذا يتحقق فيها والأقراء الحيض عندنا.

[206] Ibid., 2:274.

[c] If she is pregnant, her *'iddah* will be until she gives birth.[207]

§2. Common Scenarios where *Talaq* Occurs

<u>Cases where *Talaq* does occur:</u>

1. **Talaq for a specified time**: if a person designates a certain time for the *talaq* to come into effect, then when that time enters, *talaq* will fall, e.g. '*talaq* in 1 month's time', or '*talaq* in April!', etc.[208] (cf. 'Talaq and Condition' below).

2. **Triple Talaq but one intended**: If a man issues three *talaqs* consecutively but denies that the last two as pronouncements but merely for emphasis, then three *talaqs* will still be effective based on the legal principle: "what has a basis is given preference to what merely emphasises".[209]

3. **Talaq by letter**: this stands as it is analogous to a written pronouncement of divorce and intention is of no consideration.[210]

---

[207] Ibid., 2:274:

وإن كانت حاملا فعدتها أن تضع حملها لقوله تعالى: {وَأُولَاتُ الْأَحْمَالِ أَجَلُهُنَّ أَنْ يَضَعْنَ حَمْلَهُنَّ} الطلاق: من الآية 4

[208] Ibn 'Abidin, *Radd al-Muhtar*, 2:606.
[209] Ibn Nujaym, *al-Ashbah wa'l-Naza'ir*, p.149:

التأسيس أولى من التأكيد

[210] Ibn 'Abidin, *Radd al-Muhtar*, 3:236:

4. **Talaq by text, BBM, WhatsApp, etc.**: this stands as it is analogous to a written pronouncement of divorce.[211]

5. **Talaq by email**: this takes the same ruling as a written pronouncement of divorce.[212]

6. **Talaq by twitter**: this takes the same ruling as a written pronouncement of divorce.[213]

Note: if the *talaq* message is clearly attributed to the wife, the *talaq* falls the moment the pronouncement is written down <u>regardless of whether he has sent the message to the wife or not or whether she knows about it or not or whether she received it or not</u>.[214]

7. **Talaq by indication**: if a man utters words of divorce but does so by indication – e.g. 'daughter of so and so is divorced' or 'mother of so and so' – then

---

الكتابة علي نوعين مرسومة و غير مرسومة و نعني بالمرسومة ان يكون مصدرا و معنونا مثل ما يكتب الي الغائب و غير المرسومة ان لا يكون مصدرا و معنونا هو علي وجهين مستبينة و غير مستبينة فالمستبينة ما يكتب علي الصحيفة و الحائط و الارض علي وجه يمكن فهمه و قراءته. و ان كانت مستبينة لكنها غير مرسومة ان نوي الطلاق يقع و الا لا و ان كانت مرسومة يقع الطلاق نوي او لم ينو

[211] Ibid., 3:236.
[212] Ibid., 3:236.
[213] Ibid., 3:236.
[214] Ibid., 2:293:

كرر لفظ الطلاق وقع الكل، وإن نوى التأكيد دين .

the divorce stands. <u>It is not a condition that the wife's name be mentioned</u>.[215]

8. **Talaq by nick name**: if a woman is known by a nickname and her husband issues *talaq* to that nickname, then it stands.[216]

9. **Talaq by condition**: In general, if a husband pronounces *talaq* but ties it with a condition (*shart*), then the *talaq* will occur when that condition is fulfilled or realised. <u>Examples</u>: 'If you go to such and such place, <u>then</u> a divorce is for you!' or 'If you speak to so and so, <u>then</u> one divorce is for you!' or similar statements with similar import. If the wife goes to that place or speaks to that person then a *talaq* is effected. If the husband uses a conditional clause that carries the meaning of "otherwise"/"whenever"/"every time"/"wherever", etc. then whenever, wherever and at every time the wife does that thing, a *talaq* will occur.[217] <u>Examples</u>:

---

[215] Ibid., 3:248:

فقوله إني حلفت بالطلاق ينصرف إليها ما لم يرد غيرها لأنه يحتمله كلامه، بخلاف ما لو ذكر اسمها أو اسم أبيها أو أمها أو ولدها فقال : عمرة طالق أو بنت فلان أو بنت فلانة أو أم فلان، فقد صرحوا بأنها تطلق

[216] Ibid., 2:248f. The rule is that if an inference can be made from what is uttered to indicate the wife, then the *talaq* has an origin and hence will be effective – even if the husband denies the attribution. The rule also is that a name is not necessary for the *talaq* to be attributed, even a description of the wide would render it to have fallen.

[217] See al-Mawsili, *al-Ikhtiyar*, 1:172:

(ولو قال : أنت طالق ما لم أطلقك، أو متى ما لم أطلقك، أو متى لم أطلقك وسكت طلقت) لوجود شرط الوقوع بالسكوت، وهو زمان خال عن التطليق، لأن هذه الألفاظ للوقت، أما " متى " و " متى ما " فحقيقة فيه، وأما " ما " فإنه يستعمل فيه ، قال تعالى : (ما دمت حيا) أي وقت الحياة، (وإن قال : إن لم أطلقك،

'Whenever you lie to me, a divorce is for you!' –
Where every time the wife does tell a lie, then a
talaq will occur. (cf. 'Talaq and Promise' below).
The general rule is that unless the condition is
actually realised or fulfilled, the *talaq* will stay in
abeyance or remain suspended (*mu'allaq*).

10. **Talaq in a state of illness**: e.g. if as person is bed-
ridden or paralysed, etc. this is valid as long as a
person has control of his senses (cf. answers below).

11. **Talaq by a mentally unstable person (*ma'tuh*)**: if
the person has mental challenges (absence of *compos
mentis*) and is recorded to have a history of mental
illness then in a state of episodic insanity, his *talaq*
will not stand valid. However, when he is not in an
'episode' or mental fit, his *talaq* will stand as being
pronounced.[218] The reason being a person is not
liable before the Law due to absence of sanity.

12. **Talaq by a mentally insane person (*majnun*)**: if
the person has permanent mental disorder and is
recorded to have a history of mental illness then in
his state of insanity, his *talaq* will not stand valid.

أو إذا لم أطلقك، أو إذا ما لم أطلقك لم تطلق حتى تموت) لأن هذه الألفاظ للشرط فكان الطلاق معلقا
بعدم التعليق فلا يتحقق العدم إلا بالموت، أما " إن " فظاهر، وأما " إذا " و " إذا ما " فكذلك عنده، وقالا :
هما بمعنى " متى "، قال تعالى : (إذا السماء انشقت) وأمثالها والمراد الوقت، ولأبي حنيفة أنها تستعمل
للشرط أيضا

[218] See *al-Fatawa al-Hindiyyah*, 1:353:

وَكَذَلِكَ الْمَعْتُوهُ لَا يَقَعُ طَلَاقُهُ أَيْضًا وَهَذَا إذَا كَانَ فِي حَالَةِ الْعَتَهِ أَمَّا فِي حَالَةِ الْإِفَاقَةِ فَالصَّحِيحُ أَنَّهُ وَاقِعٌ هَكَذَا
فِي الْجَوْهَرَةِ النَّيِّرَةِ.

The reason being a person is not liable before the Law due to absence of sanity.

13. **Talaq during menses:** If a woman is in her period and the husband pronounces *talaq*, it will have occurred although the act is sinful.[219]

14. **Talaq without consummation**: If a man divorces his wife thrice even before consummation, the divorces stand and the marriage breaks down.[220]

15. **Talaq in jest**: this type counts and the *talaq* stands as pronounced.

16. **Talaq in ignorance**: this type counts and the *talaq* stands as pronounced.

17. **Talaq by mistake**: if a situation should arise that *by mistake* (e.g. he meant to say something but said a word of divorce instead) then a *talaq* stands as effected.

---

[219] Ibn al-Humam, *Fath al-Qadir*, 3:338:

وإذا طلق الرجل امرأته في حالة الحيض وقع الطلاق

It is actually an unlawful mode of divorce because it unnecessarily elongates the woman's '*iddah* period which is already a difficult time for a woman. If a *talaq* is given during this time, it is mandatory for the husband to take back the wife (*ruju'*) and then divorce her after she attains purity.

[220] See *al-Fatawa al-Hindiyyah*, 1:353:

إذا طلق الرجل امرأته ثلاثا قبل الدخول بها وقعن عليها

18. **Talaq in anger**: this type counts and the *talaq* stands as pronounced.[221]

19. **Talaq without the wife hearing it**: this type counts and the *talaq* stands as pronounced.[222]

20. **Talaq *in absentia***: if a husband divorces his wife when she is not present, the divorce stands. Her being present is not a condition for a *talaq* to occur.

21. **Talaq and witnesses**: witnesses are not a condition for the *talaq* to stand; however it is better to appoint

---

[221] Ibn 'Abidin, *Radd al-Muhtar*, 3:244:

قلت : وللحافظ ابن القيم الحنبلي رسالة في طلاق الغضبان قال فيها : إنه على ثلاثة أقسام : أحدها أن يحصل له مبادئ الغضب بحيث لا يتغير عقله ويعلم ما يقول ويقصده، وهذا لا إشكال فيه . والثاني أن يبلغ النهاية فلا يعلم ما يقول ولا يريده، فهذا لا ريب أنه لا ينفذ شيء من أقواله . الثالث من توسط بين المرتبتين بحيث لم يصر كالمجنون فهذا محل النظر، والأدلة على عدم نفوذ أقواله.ا هـ

ملخصا من شرح الغاية الحنبلية، لكن أشار في الغاية إلى مخالفته في الثالث حيث قال : ويقع الطلاق من غضب خلافا لابن القيم اهـ وهذا الموافق عندنا لما مر في المدهوش

al-Dardir, *Sharh al-Kabir*, 2:367 (Maliki text):

(أو أكره) على إيقاعه فلا يلزمه شئ في فتوى ولا قضاء لخبر مسلم: لا طلاق في إغلاق أي إكراه بل لو أكره على واحدة فأوقع أكثر فلا شئ عليه لان المكره لا يملك نفسه كالمجنون أي ولم يكن قاصدا بطلاقه حل العصمة باطنا وإلا لوقع عليه. واعلم أن الاكراه إما شرعي أو غيره، ومذهب المدونة الذي به الفتوى أن الاكراه الشرعي طوع يقع به الطلاق جزما خلافا للمغيرة، كما لو حلف بالطلاق لا خرجت زوجته فأخرجها قاض لتحلف عند المنبر، وكما لو حلف في نصف عبد يملكه لا باعه فأعتق شريكه نصفه فقوم عليه نصيب الحالف وكمل به عتق الشريك، أو حلف لا اشتراه فأعتق الحالف نصيبه فقوم عليه نصيب شريكه لتكميل عتقه لزمه الطلاق على المذهب،

[222] Mufti Lajpuri, *al-Fatawa al-Rahimiyyah*, 8:266.

witnesses in order to avoid disputes and for evidence in court which will rely on witness testimony.[223]

22. **Talaq and mispronunciation**: If a person mispronounces the word <*talaq*>, e.g. the letter 't/ط' as 'd/د', or the letter 'q/ق' as 'gh/غ' [as in *talagh, dalaq*, [طلاغ/دلاق] etc.], then *talaq* will still occur.[224]

23. **Talaq and intoxication**: if a man issues *talaq* in a state of intoxication (e.g. drunk due to alcohol, under the influence of drugs, etc.) then according to the Hanafi School it stands as having occurred.[225]

** **Remember**: If the above cases are where the husband pronounces **three times** in one sitting, session, gathering,

---

[223] Zafar Usmani, *I'la' al-Sunan*, 11:204.

[224] *al-Fatawa al-Hindiyyah*, 1:357:

رجل قال لامرأته ترا تلاق .هاهنا خمسة ألفاظ. تلاق وتلاغ وطلاغ وطلاك وتلاك عن الشيخ الإمام الجليل أبي بكر محمد بن الفضل رحمه الله تعالى أنه يقع وإن تعمد وقصد أن لا يقع ولا يصدق قضاء ويصدق ديانة إلا إذا أشهد قبل أن يتلفظ به وقال إن امرأتي تطلب مني الطلاق ولا ينبغي لي أن أطلقها فأتلفظ بها قطعا لقيلها وتلفظ بها وشهدوا بذلك عند الحاكم لا يحكم بالطلاق بينهما وكان في الابتداء يفرق بين العالم والجاهل كما هو جواب شمس الأئمة الحلواني – رحمه الله تعالى – ثم رجع إلى ما قلنا وعليه الفتوى كذا في الخلاصة

[225] Ibn 'Abidin, *Radd al-Muhtar*, 3:239:

وَبَيَّنَ في التَّحْرِيرِ حُكْمَهُ أَنَّهُ إنْ كَانَ سُكْرُهُ بِطَرِيقٍ مُحَرَّمٍ لَا يُبْطِلُ تَكْلِيفَهُ فَتَلْزَمُهُ الْأَحْكَامُ وَتَصِحُّ عِبَارَتُهُ مِنْ الطَّلَاقِ وَالْعَتَاقِ، وَالْبَيْعِ وَالْإِقْرَارِ، وَتَزْوِيجِ الصِّغَارِ مِنْ كُفْءٍ، وَالْإِقْرَاضِ وَالِاسْتِقْرَاضِ لِأَنَّ الْعَقْلَ قَائِمٌ، وَإِنَّمَا عَرَضَ فَوَاتُ فَهْمِ الْخِطَابِ بِمَعْصِيَتِهِ، فَبَقِيَ في حَقِّ الْإِثْمِ وَوُجُوبِ الْقَضَاءِ، وَيَصِحُّ إسْلَامُهُ كَالْمُكْرَهِ لِإِرَادَتِهِ لِعَدَمِ الْقَصْدِ

encounter, meeting or time and place *simultaneously*, then an immediate irretrievable divorce has taken place, i.e. the husband and wife are separated permanently.[226]

§3. Common Scenarios where Talaq does not Occur

Cases where *Talaq* does not occur:

1. **Talaq by coercion**: If a person is forced to write a *talaq* (resulting in loss of life or limb) then it will not occur. However, if he utters it then even if he does not intend it, the *talaq* will still legally stand.[227]

---

[226] Shaykh Zadah, *Majma' al-Anhur*, 2:88:

(وَلَا تَحِلُّ الْحُرَّةُ بَعْدَ) الطَّلَقَاتِ (الثَّلَاثِ) لِمُطَلِّقِهَا لِقَوْلِهِ تَعَالَى {فَإِنْ طَلَّقَهَا فَلَا تَحِلُّ لَهُ مِنْ بَعْدُ} [البقرة: 230] الْآيَةَ (وَلَا الْأَمَةُ بَعْدَ الثِّنْتَيْنِ) لِمَا تَقَرَّرَ أَنَّ الرِّقَّ مُنَصِّفٌ وَالطَّلْقَةَ لَا تَتَجَزَّأُ (إِلَّا بَعْدَ وَطْءِ زَوْجٍ آخَرَ) سَوَاءٌ كَانَ حُرًّا أَوْ عَبْدًا زُوِّجَ بِإِذْنِ الْمَوْلَى عَاقِلًا أَوْ كَانَ مَجْنُونًا إِذَا كَانَ يُجَامِعُ مِثْلَهُ مُسْلِمًا أَوْ ذِمِّيًّا فِي الذِّمِّيَّةِ حَتَّى يَحِلَّهَا لِزَوْجِهَا الْمُسْلِمِ (بِنِكَاحٍ صَحِيحٍ) فَيَخْرُجُ الْفَاسِدُ وَنِكَاحُ غَيْرِ الْكُفْوِ إِذَا كَانَ لَهَا وَلِيٌّ عَلَى مَا عَلَيْهِ الْفَتْوَى وَالنِّكَاحُ الْمَوْقُوفُ (وَمُضِيِّ عِدَّتِهِ)

[227] Ibn 'Abidin, *Radd al-Muhtar*, 3:235-236:

وفي البحر أن المراد الإكراه على التلفظ بالطلاق، فلو أكره على أن يكتب طلاق امرأته فكتب لا تطلق لأن الكتابة أقيمت مقام العبارة باعتبار الحاجة ولا حاجة هنا، كذا في الخانية

al-Bukhari, *al-Muhit al-Burhani*, 3:528:

وفي «فتاوى أهل سمرقند»: إذا أكره الرجل بالحبس والضرب على أن يكتب طلاق امرأته فكتب فلانة بنت فلان طالق لا تطلق لأن الكتاب من الغائب جعل بمنزلة الخطاب من الحاضر باعتبار الحاجة، ولا حاجة ههنا حيث احتيج إلى الضرب والله أعلم

2. **Talaq and extreme pressure**: if a man is pressured to sign a divorce paper (due to emotional blackmail, harm, etc. [= *ghayr mulji'*]) and he does not want a divorce, then no divorce will occur.[228]

3. **Talaq in a dream**: *Talaq* pronounced in a dream does not occur.[229]

4. **Talaq to one's self**: if a husband merely repeats the words <*talaq*> to himself, then no divorce occurs on his wife.

5. **Talaq and thinking**: merely thinking about *talaq* does not have any legal effects. Utterance is legally taken into consideration only.[230]

6. **Talaq in a whisper**: majority of scholars hold that *talaq* has to be heard, i.e. it is sufficiently audible for the one who pronounced it.[231]

---

[228] Ibid., 3:528.

[229] Ibn 'Abidin, *Radd al-Muhtar*, 3:242-243.

[230] al-Shurunbulali, *Maraqi al-Falah*, p.219:

حتى لو أجرى الطلاق على قلبه وحرك لسانه من غير تلفظ يسمع لا يقع

Ibn 'Abidin, *Radd al-Muhtar*, 3:320:

(قوله وركنه لفظ مخصوص) هو ما جعل دلالة على معنى الطلاق من صريح أو كناية فخرج الفسوخ على ما مر، وأراد اللفظ ولو حكما ليدخل الكتابة المستبينة وإشارة الأخرس والإشارة إلى العدد بالأصابع في قوله أنت طالق هكذا كما سيأتي . وبه ظهر أن من تشاجر مع زوجته فأعطاها ثلاثة أحجار ينوي الطلاق ولم يذكر لفظا لا صريحا ولا كناية لا يقع عليه كما أفتى به الخير الرملي وغيره، وكذا ما يفعله بعض سكان البوادي من أمرها بحلق شعرها لا يقع به طلاق وإن نواه

[231] al-Sarakhsi, *al-Mabsut*, 3:2:

7. **Talaq and fainting**: theoretically, a person fainting and issuing *talaq* does not stand as he has diminished reasoning powers at that point.[232]

أن من أقر بطلاق سابق يكون ذلك إيقاعا منه في الحال؛ لأن من ضرورة الاستناد الوقوع في الحال، وهو مالك للإيقاع غير مالك للإسناد

ولو أقر بالطلاق كاذبا أو هازلا وقع قضاء لا ديانة... كما لو أقر بالطلاق هازلا أو كاذبا فقال في البحر، وإن مراده لعدم الوقوع في المشبه به عدمه ديانة، ثم نقل عن البزازية والقنية لو أراد به الخبر عن الماضي كذبا لا يقع ديانة، وإن أشهد قبل ذلك لا يقع قضاء أيضا

Ibn 'Abidin, *Radd al-Muhtar*, 1:534f:

(و) أدنى (الجهر إسماع غيره و) أدنى (المخافتة إسماع نفسه) ومن بقربه

(قوله وأدنى الجهر إسماع غيره إلخ) اعلم أنهم اختلفوا في حد وجود القراءة على ثلاثة أقوال : فشرط الهندواني والفضلي لوجودها خروج صوت يصل إلى أذنه، وبه قال الشافعي .
وشرط بشر المريسي وأحمد خروج الصوت من الفم وإن لم يصل إلى أذنه ، لكن بشرط كونه مسموعا في الجملة ، حتى لو أدنى أحد صماخه إلى فيه يسمع .
ولم يشترط الكرخي وأبو بكر البلخي السماع، واكتفيا بتصحيح الحروف .
واختار شيخ الإسلام وقاضي خان وصاحب المحيط والحلواني قول الهندواني، وكذا في معراج الدراية .
ونقل في المجتبى عن الهندواني أنه لا يجزيه ما لم تسمع أذناه ومن بقربه، وهذا لا يخالف ما مر عن الهندواني لأن ما كان مسموعا له يكون مسموعا لمن في قربه كما في الحلية والبحر .
وذكر أن كلا من قولي الهندواني والكرخي مصححان، وأن ما قاله الهندواني أصح وأرجح لاعتماد أكثر علمائنا عليه .
فقد ظهر بهذا أن أدنى المخافتة إسماع نفسه أو من بقربه من رجل أو رجلين مثلا، وأعلاها تصحيح الحروف كما هو مذهب الكرخي، ولا تعتبر هنا في الأصح .
(ويجري ذلك) المذكور (في كل ما يتعلق بنطق، كتسمية على ذبيحة ووجوب سجدة تلاوة وعتاق وطلاق واستثناء) وغيرها؛ فلو طلق أو استثنى ولم يسمع نفسه لم يصح في الأصح
(قوله ويجري ذلك المذكور) يعني كون أدنى ما يتحقق به الكلام إسماع نفسه أو من بقربه
(قوله لم يصح في الأصح) أي الذي هو قول الهندواني.

[232] Ibid., 3:586:

8. **Talaq while asleep**: this does not have any legal consequences because no intention was made and one is not held accountable while asleep..

9. **Talaq and teaching**: if a person is teaching *fiqh* and uses phrases like 'I divorce my wife', 'you are divorced' purely for instructional purposes, then no *talaq* occurs.[233]

10. **Talaq under *waswasah***: being under the influence of satanic whisperings does not have any legal effect because no real intention is involved to divorce and this can be confirmed – as a protective measure – if a person states before two witnesses that his pronouncements of divorce are not from him but internal whisperings and insinuation.

11. **Talaq and mere intent**: merely intending *talaq* does not actualise a *talaq*.

12. **Talaq and promise**: if a person says to his wife, 'I will divorce you', or 'I swear by God I'll divorce you!' then no divorce occurs. This is because it is a promise to divorce and not an actual pronouncement of divorce. Hence, future statements of divorce are not upheld.[234]

---

[233] Ibid., 3:250:

(قوله أو لم ينو شيئا) لما مر أن الصريح لا يحتاج إلى النية، ولكن لا بد في وقوعه قضاء وديانة من قصد إضافة لفظ الطلاق إليها عالما بمعناه ولم يصرفه إلى ما يحتمله كما أفاده في الفتح، وحققه في النهر، احترازا عما لو كرر مسائل الطلاق بحضرتها، أو كتب ناقلا من كتاب امرأتي طالق مع التلفظ، أو حكى يمين غيره فإنه لا يقع أصلا ما لم يقصد زوجته

[234] Ibid., 3:248:

13. **Talaq and ignorance**: If a man does not know the meaning or import of the words he utters in *talaq*, then it will not be effective (e.g. if he were to keep repeating the word <*talaq*> but did not know its import).[235]

14. **Talaq by a woman**: a woman saying <*talaq*> to her husband has no legal consequences because *talaq* is effected by a man.

15. **Talaq and doubts**: if one doubts whether he pronounced *talaq*, then the level of doubt must be ascertained. If he genuinely had doubts (i.e. he really cannot remember), then that would be taken into consideration and hence no divorce would have occurred. This is because what one is certain of cannot be overridden by mere doubt.[236] However, if one has a greater thought that one did issue or pronounce a divorce, the divorce having occurred would be considered. This is because *zann al-ghalib*

و كذا المضارع اذا غلب فى الحال مثل اطلقك كما فى البحر

[235] Ibid., 3:250:

وعما لو لقنته لفظ الطلاق فتلفظ به غير عالم بمعناه فلا يقع أصلا على ما أفتى به مشايخ أوزجند صيانة عن التلبيس وغيرهم من الوقوع قضاء فقط

[236] Mulla Khusru, *Durar al-Hukkam*, 1:20:

ما ثبت بيقين لا يرتفع بالشك وما ثبت بيقين لا يرتفع إلا بيقين

(prevailing assumption/strong presumption) takes the ruling of certainty.[237]

16. **Talaq and useless talk**: if a man directs his pronouncement of *talaq* to parts of the human body – e.g. '*talaq* to your hands!' or '*talaq* to your hair!' – then this will not stand as it will be considered nonsense and useless talk.

---

[237] Ibid., 1:20:

وأما إذا كان القلب يطمئن للجهة الراجحة فتكون (ظنا غالبا) والظن الغالب ينزل منزلة اليقين .

Chapter 9: "Mutual Terms and Custody: *Important Post-Talaq Responsibilities*"

———— T ————

§1. General Responsibilities

- After a divorce, it is imperative that the separated families behave with:

1. The utmost maturity.
2. Respect and etiquette.
3. Tolerance.
4. Kindness.
5. Fairness.
6. Understanding.
7. *Taqwa* (Allah-consciousness).

All too often, a divorce brings out the most un-Islamic traits of a person and this is very unfortunate. Separation should be amicable as this is the aim of the Shariah. Each person must be accepting of the situation and learn to afford the other their Shariah given rights and think of the child and its future. Hence, the rights of the children must never be overlooked. These rights of the child generally include:[238]

---

[238] The Prophet said: **"...and your children have rights too..."** (Muslim, *Sahih* (#1159).

... وإن لولدك عليك حقاً

al-Munawi in *Fayd al-Qadir*, 2:574 states: "Just as your parents have rights over you, so too your child has rights over you, rather many rights, such as teaching them the individual obligations, teaching them

[1] <u>Before birth:</u>

1. The right to be given an Islamic name.[239]
2. The right of *tahnik* (touching the lips of a new born with something sweet; usually by a pious person).[240]

Islamic manners, giving them gifts equally, whether that is a gift, a *waqf* (endowment), or other gift. If preference is shown with no reason, that is regarded as invalid by some of the scholars and as *makruh* (disliked) by others."

كما أن لوالديك عليك حقا كذلك لولدك عليك حقا أي حقوقا كثيرة منها تعليمهم الفروض العينية وتأديبهم بالآداب الشرعية والعدل بينهم في العطية سواء كانت هبة أم هدية أم وقفا أم تبرعا آخر فإن فَضَّل بلا عذر بطل عند بعض العلماء وكره عند بعضهم

[239] Ibn Qayyim al-Jawziyyah writes in *Tuhfat al-Mawlud*, p.111: "The purpose of naming [something] is to define the thing named because if there is something whose name is unknown it is difficult to refer to it. So it is permissible to name [the child] on the day he is born and it is permissible to delay the naming until the third day, or until the day of the 'aqiqah, or before or after that. The matter is broad in scope…"

إن التسمية لما كانت حقيقتها تعريف الشيء المسمى لأنه إذا وجد وهو مجهول الاسم لم يكن له ما يقع تعريفه به فجاز تعريفه يوم وجوده وجاز تأخير التعريف إلى ثلاثة أيام وجاز إلى يوم العقيقة عنه ويجوز قبل ذلك وبعده والأمر فيه واسع . "

[240] al-Nawawi states in his commentary on the *Sahih* of Imam Muslim, 14:122-123: "The scholars are agreed that it is *mustahabb* (preferred) to do *tahnik* with dates for the child when he is born; if that is not possible then to use some similar kind of sweet. The dates should be chewed until they become soft enough to be swallowed, then the child's mouth should be opened and a little of the dates put in his mouth…"

اتفق العلماء على استحباب تحنيك المولود عند ولادته بتمر فإن تعذر فما في معناه وقريب منه من الحلو فيمضغ المحنّك التمر حتى تصير مائعة بحيث تبتلع ثم يفتح فم المولود ويضعها فيه ليدخل شيء منها جوفه

[2] <u>After birth:</u>

3. The right for an *'aqiqah* (a sacrificial slaughter on the occasion of a new born).[241]
4. The right to be cared for and loved.
5. The right to fair treatment.
6. The right to necessities (food, clothing, shelter, etc. = §3. below).
7. The right to be Islamically educated (*tarbiyyah*: in the basic religious instruction and knowledge like praying, fasting, purity, buying and selling, etc.).[242]
8. The right to be trained in proper etiquette and good character.[243]

---

[241] Abu Dawud, *Sunan* (#2838):

غلام رهينة بعقيقته تذبح عنه يوم سابعه ويحلق ويسمى

[242] Bukhari, *Sahih* (#2416): "Each of you is a shepherd and is responsible for his flock. The ruler who is in charge of people is a shepherd and is responsible for them. The man is the shepherd of his household and is responsible for them. The woman is the shepherd of her husband's house and child and is responsible for them. The slave is the shepherd of his master's wealth and is responsible for it. Each of you is a shepherd and each of you is responsible for his flock…"

كلكم راع فمسؤول عن رعيته فالأمير الذي على الناس راع وهو مسؤول عنهم والرجل راع على أهل بيته وهو مسؤول عنهم والمرأة راعية على بيت بعلها وولده وهي مسؤولة عنهم والعبد راع على مال سيده وهو مسؤول عنه ألا فكلكم راع وكلكم مسؤول عن رعيته

[243] al-Nawawi, *Sharh Sahih Muslim*, 8:44: "The father must discipline his child and teach him what he needs to know of religious duties. This teaching is obligatory upon the father and all those in charge of children before the child reaches the age of adolescence. This was stated by al-Shafi'i and his companions. al-Shafi'i and his companions said: This teaching is also obligatory upon the mother, if there is no father, because it is part of the child's upbringing and they have a share of that and the wages for this teaching may be taken from the child's own wealth. If the

After a divorce, the child maintains certain of these rights and the efforts must be strongly collaborative in ensuring they are realised:

1. Maintenance (see below, §3.).
2. Love and care.
3. Fair treatment.
4. Islamic upbringing (*tarbiyyah*).

Some related rulings:

- It is not permitted to exploit a child in a post-divorce battle (e.g. for psychological abuse, blackmail, etc.).
- It is not permitted to *emotionally* harm each other post-divorce (e.g. defame, slander, expose, etc.).
- It is not permitted to *physically* harm each other post-divorce (e.g. hire thugs to attack, hit-men, etc.)
- It is not permitted to take revenge on one's ex-partner in any shape or form.

§2. Child Custody

A divorce scenario raises issues of child custody rights, i.e. who will take responsibility for the child's care

---

child has no wealth then the one who is obliged to spend on him may spend on his education, because it is one of the things that he needs. And Allah knows best."

على الأب تأديب ولده وتعليمه ما يحتاج إليه من وظائف الدين وهذا التعليم واجب على الأب وسائر الأولياء قبل بلوغ الصبي والصبية نص عليه الشافعي وأصحابه ، قال الشافعي وأصحابه : وعلى الأمهات أيضا هذا التعليم إذا لم يكن أب لأنه من باب التربية ولهن مدخل في ذلك وأجرة هذا التعليم في مال الصبي فإن لم يكن له مال فعلى من تلزمه نفقته لأنه مما يحتاج إليه والله أعلم

and responsibilities. This is known in Arabic as *"hadanah"* (حضانة) which comes from the root *h / d / n /* meaning 'to take a child', 'to put a child in one's bosom' and 'to take care of a child'.[244] The Shariah has arranged defined custody durations for both the mother and father. Below is a general outline of the rulings related to custody law in the Shariah:[245]

If the child is a boy:

- The mother has custody rights to the boy until he reaches the age of approximately 7 years (or when he is able to eat, drink and dress by himself).
- The father has right of custody from the age of 7 until the child reaches the age of maturity (*bulugh*).
- Legally speaking, once a child reaches the age of puberty, he can choose who he wants to live with or even live independently.[246]

---

[244] Lane, *Lexicon*, Bk. 1, pp.501-502.
[245] See also:

1. http://fiqh.huquq.com/2012/02/custody-al-hadanah.html
2. http://www.daruliftaa.com/question?txt_QuestionID=q-13384872
3. http://www.sunniforum.com/forum/showthread.php?82209-Child-Custody
4. http://spa.qibla.com/issue_view.asp?HD=12&ID=168&CATE=11

[246] See *al-Fatawa al-Hindiyyah*, 1:566:

وَالْأُمُّ وَالْجَدَّةُ أَحَقُّ بِالْغُلَامِ حَتَّى يَسْتَغْنِيَ وَقُدِّرَ بِسَبْعِ سِنِينَ وَقَالَ الْقُدُورِيُّ حَتَّى يَأْكُلَ وَحْدَهُ وَيَشْرَبَ وَحْدَهُ وَيَسْتَنْجِيَ وَحْدَهُ وَقَدَّرَهُ أَبُو بَكْرٍ الرَّازِيّ بِتِسْعِ سِنِينَ وَالْفَتْوَى عَلَى الْأَوَّلِ وَالْأُمُّ وَالْجَدَّةُ أَحَقُّ بِالْجَارِيَةِ حَتَّى تَحِيضَ وَفِي نَوَادِرِ هِشَامٍ عَنْ مُحَمَّدٍ رَحِمَهُ اللَّهُ تَعَالَى إِذَا بَلَغَتْ حَدَّ الشَّهْوَةِ فَالْأَبُ أَحَقُّ وَهَذَا صَحِيحٌ هَكَذَا

If the child is a girl:

- The mother has custody rights from birth until puberty (approximately 9 years of age).[247]

فِي التَّبْيِينِ . وَبَعْدَمَا اسْتَغْنَى الْغُلَامُ وَبَلَغَتْ الْجَارِيَةُ فَالْعَصَبَةُ أَوْلَى يُقَدَّمُ الْأَقْرَبُ فَالْأَقْرَبُ كَذَا فِي فَتَاوَى قَاضِي خَانْ.

وَيُمْسِكُهُ هَؤُلَاءِ إنْ كَانَ غُلَامًا إلَى أَنْ يُدْرِكَ فَبَعْدَ ذَلِكَ يُنْظَرُ إنْ كَانَ قَدْ اجْتَمَعَ رَأْيُهُ وَهُوَ مَأْمُونٌ عَلَى نَفْسِهِ يُخَلَّى سَبِيلُهُ فَيَذْهَبُ حَيْثُ شَاءَ ، وَإِنْ كَانَ غَيْرَ مَأْمُونٍ عَلَى نَفْسِهِ فَالْأَبُ يَضُمُّهُ إلَى نَفْسِهِ وَيُوَلِّيهِ وَلَا نَفَقَةَ عَلَيْهِ إلَّا إذَا تَطَوَّعَ كَذَا فِي شَرْحِ الطَّحَاوِيِّ.

[247] See Mulla Khusru, *al-Durar al-Hukkam*, 1:411:

وَ (الْأُمُّ وَالْجَدَّةُ أَحَقُّ بِهَا) أَيْ بِالصَّبِيَّةِ مِنْ الْأَبِ (حَتَّى تَحِيضَ) لِأَنَّهَا بَعْدَ الِاسْتِغْنَاءِ تَحْتَاجُ إِلَى مَعْرِفَةِ آدَابِ النِّسَاءِ، وَالْمَرْأَةُ عَلَى ذَلِكَ أَقْدَرُ وَبَعْدَ الْبُلُوغِ تَحْتَاجُ إِلَى التَّحْصِينِ وَالْحِفْظِ وَالْأَبُ فِيهِ أَقْدَرُ

al-Haskafi, *Durr al-Mukhtar*, 3:566:

وَالْأُمُّ وَالْجَدَّةُ لِأُمٍّ، أَوْ لِأَبٍ (أَحَقُّ بِهَا) بِالصَّغِيرَةِ (حَتَّى تَحِيضَ) أَيْ تَبْلُغَ فِي ظَاهِرِ الرِّوَايَةِ

al-Mawsili, *al-Ikhtiyar li-Ta'lil al-Mukhtar*, 4:15:

قَالَ: (وَتَكُونُ الْجَارِيَةُ عِنْدَ الْأُمِّ وَالْجَدَّةِ حَتَّى تَحِيضَ وَعِنْدَ غَيْرِهِمَا حَتَّى تَسْتَغْنِيَ)

al-Zayla'i, *Tabyin al-Haqa'iq*, 3:49:

(وَبِهَا حَتَّى تَحِيضَ) أَيْ الْأُمُّ وَالْجَدَّةُ أَحَقُّ بِالْجَارِيَةِ حَتَّى تَحِيضَ لِأَنَّ بَعْدَ الِاسْتِغْنَاءِ تَحْتَاجُ إِلَى مَعْرِفَةِ آدَابِ النِّسَاءِ مِنْ الْغَزْلِ وَالطَّبْخِ وَالْغَسْلِ، وَالْأُمُّ أَقْدَرُ عَلَى ذَلِكَ فَإِذَا بَلَغَتْ تَحْتَاجُ إِلَى التَّزْوِيجِ وَالصِّيَانَةِ، وَإِلَى الْأَبِ وِلَايَةُ التَّزْوِيجِ، وَهُوَ أَقْدَرُ عَلَى الصِّيَانَةِ، وَهَذَا لِأَنَّهَا صَارَتْ عُرْضَةً لِلْفِتْنَةِ، وَمَطْمَعًا لِلرِّجَالِ، وَبِالرِّجَالِ مِنْ الْغَيْرَةِ مَا لَيْسَ بِالنِّسَاءِ فَالْأَبُ أَقْدَرُ عَلَى دَفْعِ خِدَاعِ الْفَسَقَةِ وَاحْتِيَالِهِمْ فَكَانَ أَوْلَى، وَفِي نَوَادِرِ هِشَامٍ عَنْ مُحَمَّدٍ إذَا بَلَغَتْ حَدَّ الشَّهْوَةِ فَالْأَبُ أَحَقُّ بِهَا، وَهَذَا صَحِيحٌ لِمَا ذَكَرْنَا مِنْ الْحَاجَةِ إِلَى الصِّيَانَةِ، وَبِهِ يُفْتَى فِي زَمَانِنَا لِكَثْرَةِ الْفُسَّاقِ، وَإِذَا بَلَغَتْ إحْدَى عَشْرَةَ سَنَةً فَقَدْ بَلَغَتْ حَدَّ الشَّهْوَةِ فِي قَوْلِهِمْ وَقَدَّرَهُ أَبُو اللَّيْثِ بِتِسْعِ سِنِينَ، وَعَلَيْهِ الْفَتْوَى

- The father has transferred custody from puberty until her marriage (as guardian).[248]

<u>Third party custody</u>:

- The initial right of custody will be taken away from the mother if she:

1) Leaves Islam (i.e. apostatizes),

2) Openly indulges in sins such as adultery and there is a fear of the child being affected,

3) She does not attend to the child due to her leaving the house very often,

4) She marries a non-relative (stranger) to the child by which the child may be adversely affected,

5) She demands payment for the upbringing of the child if there is another woman to raise the child without remuneration.

---

al-Babarti, *al-'Inayah Sharh al-Hidayah*, 4:372:

وَحَدُّ الشَّهْوَةِ أَنْ تَبْلُغَ إِحْدَى عَشْرَةَ سَنَةً فِي قَوْلِهِمْ، كَذَا فِي النِّهَايَةِ. وَقَالَ الْفَقِيهُ أَبُو اللَّيْثِ: حَدُّ الشَّهْوَةِ أَنْ تَبْلُغَ تِسْعَ سِنِينَ، وَقِيلَ إِذَا بَلَغَتْ سِتَّ سِنِينَ أَوْ سَبْعًا أَوْ ثَمَانٍ إِنْ كَانَتْ عَبْلَةً

[248] Qudri Paşa, *al-Ahkam al-Shar'iyyah*, art.352 and 494-495:

وتنتهي مدة حضانة الصبية ببلوغها تسع سنين

Related scenarios in this context will be:

1. If the mother is unable to arrange support and care for the child (e.g. if she is an alcoholic, drug abuser, wayward, disinterested, etc.) the custody will be transferred to a third party.
2. Death.
3. Wayward behaviour (e.g. behaviour not in the interest or safety of the child).
4. Mentally challenged (e.g. dementia, deep depression, suicidal, insanity, etc.).

- The Shariah has given third party custody to the child in the following order of relations (*al-aqarib*):

(ذوي الأرحام/*dhuwi 'l-arham*):

1. Maternal grandmother and ascending;
2. Paternal grandmother and ascending;
3. Full sisters,
4. Maternal half sisters,
5. Paternal half sisters,
6. Maternal aunts,
7. Paternal aunts.

After all the avenues of the female relatives have been exhausted as explained by the Jurists, the males have the right of custody in the following sequence:

(عصبة/*'asabah*):

1. Father,
2. Paternal grandfather,
3. Real brother,

4. Paternal brother,
5. Maternal brother.

The general reason why the child is put into the custody of the mother or other female relatives during the pre-puberty years is because they are best suited for that role due to their natural inclinations of kindness, care, love and gentleness. This is also because of the natural attachment the child has with the mother and vice-versa.[249] They are also best placed to rear the child and educate it; more so than the father (and male relatives) who has obligations placed on him to ensure the maintenance of the house which is external to the internal domestic realities.[250] As for the case of the father and custody post-puberty years, this is because the male child is required to learn skills of responsibility as well as masculine traits in order to then take on his own independent responsibilities and the female child transfers to the protection of the father who becomes her legal guardian and responsible for her protection and overall well-being.

Related rulings:

- If a woman remarries another man who is not related to her child, then she forfeits her right to custody to a third party. This is because in a new marriage, her

---

[249] al-Zuhayli, *al-Fiqh al-Islam wa Adillatuhu*, 10:298:

الأم أحق بحضانة الولد بعد الفرقة بطلاق أو وفاة بالأجماع لوفور شفقتها

[250] al-Sarghirji, *al-Fiqh al-Hanafi wa Adillatuhu*, 2:261:

وفوض التربية الى النساء لأنهن أشفق واحني واقدر علي التربية من الرجال واقوي

primary duties will be to her husband who also may not want direct responsibility for her child (which is his right). This could impede full and proper care of the child and so next of kin/third party custody would be optimal.[251]

- It is not permitted to prevent a person visitation rights to see h/her child. This is a serious sin.
- It is not permitted to disappear or escape away with one's child without notifying the other parent.
- It is not permitted to abduct any child.
- It is not permitted to ransom any child for revenge purposes.
- It is permitted to mutually agree visitation times.[252]
- It is permitted for ex-couples to meet with their children although the Shariah guidelines will have to

---

[251] Based on the *hadith* narrated by Abu Dawud, al-Bayhaqi and al-Hakim: "A woman said: 'O Messenger of Allah, my womb was a vessel to this son of mine, my bosoms a water-skin for him, and my lap a gathering-place for him, yet his father has divorced me and wants to take him away from me. The Messenger of Allah said: **'You have more right to him as long as you do not marry'**…'"

أن امرأة قالت يا رسول الله إن ابني هذا كان بطني له وعاء وثديي له سقاء وحجري له حواء وإن أباه طلقني وأراد أن ينتزعه مني فقال لها رسول الله صلى الله عليه وسلم أنت أحق به ما لم تنكحي

[252] See al-Zuhayli, *al-Fiqh al-Islami*, 7:740:

حق الرؤية أو الزيارة لأحد الأبوين غير الحاضن مقرر شرعاً باتفاق الفقهاء، لصلة الرحم، ولكنهم ذكروا آراء مختلفة نسبياً، بحسب تقدير المصلحة لكل من الولد والوالد الذي يكون ولده في حضانة غيره.

قال الحنفية : إذا كان الولد عند الحاضنة، فلأبيه حق رؤيته، بأن تخرج الصغير إلى مكان يمكن الأب أن يراه فيه كل يوم. وإذا كان الولد عند أبيه لسقوط حق الأم في الحضانة، أو لانتهاء مدة الحضانة، فلأمه رؤيته، بأن يخرجه إلى مكان يمكنها أن تبصر ولدها، كل يوم. والحد الأقصى كل أسبوع مرة كحق المرأة في زيارة أبويها، والخالة مثل الأم، ولكن كما جرى القضاء في مصر، تكون زيارتها كل شهر مرة.

be observed because each is legally a stranger to the other.

- It is permitted to plan the child's future together but again Shariah guidelines will have to be observed in doing this.
- If a mother is non-Muslim, the child custody still automatically transfers to her until puberty. However, if they begin to discern religious ideas, then because of fear of disbelief (*kufr*) the matter will be investigated.

§3. Maintenance

Expenses of the child are one of h/her rights. It is the father's legal responsibility.[253] The mother has no legal obligation of expenses for her children even if she is working.

Related rulings:

- If the ex-wife has no apartment to live or is unable to find accommodation, the ex-husband must arrange the living expenses.
- Each child must be treated fairly and given expenses fairly.
- The necessities must be provided for in the expenses: food, clothing and shelter.

---

[253] al-Marghinani, *al-Hidayah*, 2:434:

وإذا وقعت الفرقة ين الزوجين فالأم أحق بالولد لما روى أن امرأة قالت يا رسول الله إن ابني هذا كان بطني له وعاء وحجري له حواء وثديي له سقاء وزعم أبوه أنه ينزعه مني فقال عليه الصلاة والسلام أنت أحق به مالم تتزوجي ولأن الأم أشفق وأقدر على الحضانة ... والنفقة على الأب على ما نذكر ولا تجبر الأم عليه لأنها عست تعجز عن الحضانة.

- The expenses are determined by local customs and standards and so will vary from country to country.
- Any child credit or financial support from the state although helpful to the child will not absolve the father of his responsibility to maintain their expenses.
- If the income of the father is through unlawful means, then the wife and children receiving the money will be permitted to take it. The sin will fall on the father.

Chapter 10: "Four Wives and All That: *Responding to Some Misconceptions about Marriage and Divorce in Islam*"

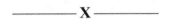

§.1 Intellectual Basis

Whenever an argument is to be understood, assessed and explained, the intellectual basis from which a Muslim proceeds is very important. Islam's basis is **rational**, i.e. built on intellectual arguments that are concrete. The basis of the Islamic belief is:

1. **Belief in God (Allah).**
   —— God is the only plausible cause of the Universe.
   —— Design in the world indicates an intelligent designer.

2. **Belief in the Divine word of God (the Qur'an).**
   —— An Arab could not have authored the Qur'an.
   —— A non-Arab could not have authored the Qur'an.
   —— The Qur'anic challenge has not been met which is historically recorded.
   —— The Qur'an is beyond the productive capacity of human beings (e.g. there are no mistakes, its inexhaustible meaning, etc.).

3. **Belief in the need for Messengers and Prophets.**
   —— If there is a God and the Qur'an is the word of God then there needs to be individuals who

practically exemplify the divine message so it is emulated by others.

If the above are true and correct, then *whatever is established from this basis is also true and correct.*

Some wider points to consider:

1. Even if we can't understand a ruling from Allah, it doesn't mean there's no wisdom behind it.

2. Even if a ruling from Allah seems difficult to accept, this may not be due to the ruling itself but our distorted perceptions and prejudices or our cultural upbringing.

3. Even if we cannot explain a ruling, we trust that given the way Allah is as our Creator, there is a general benefit for human beings in that ruling.

4. Whatever the ruling of Allah is, it is not legislated based on a gender bias, antagonism towards one sex over another, hatred or discrimination, i.e. are not the reasons.

5. Islamic sources are not to be interpreted through a hermeneutic prism that assumes imperialist categories or western standards removed form Islamic frames of reference.

Below will be examination of areas within the Shariah related to the domestic interaction that are seen as difficult and untenable. They are often portrayed in the media and maligned without regard for proper terms of fair debate and honest, mature and intellectual discussion:

1.

'Four wives so why not four husbands!'

[P1] A man is allowed to marry up to four wives.
[P2] Women are not allowed to marry four husbands.

_____

[C1] *Therefore*, the Shariah is unfair for women.

Response 1:

- Polygyny (i.e. a man in marriage with more than one woman) is legally **allowed** in Islam.
- Polygyny is not obligatory but merely permissible based on certain conditions: e.g. fair treatment between wives and justice. Islam does not force, oblige or even encourage men to enter polygamous marriages.
- Polygyny is not a 'lesser marriage' but an **equally valid, fulfilling and rewarding marriage** as a monogamous marriage (this point is often misinterpreted and misunderstood).
- Western propaganda against polygyny clouds impartial and fair assessment of the Islamic positon (e.g. by misrepresenting the Islamic stance on the issue and thus affects peoples' perception of it).

- **Some wisdoms (*hikam*) and broader benefits (*manafi'*) behind legislating polygyny:**

1. *The problem of unmarried women*: should they not be entitled to a marriage, family life and companionship with a life partner? What about elderly women, are they not entitled to build a family? Polygyny offers a means by which to gain fulfilment in a loving marriage and relationship and thus self-fulfilment.

2. *Reduced male population*: what about scenarios where there are fewer men in a given population – especially after wars were many men die. Or what about high imprisonment % of males that creates a social problem and therefore the ratio of men to women is disproportionate (imbalanced sex ratio). What should be done? Polygyny helps relieve this social imbalance in the society by offering women a means to building a family and relationship by marrying an already married man.

   • Given this context above, does the claim of Shariah unfairness remain as strong and effective? No. **Question**: Is it unfair for a woman to seek a male companion as a legal life-partner or seek a family, a marriage and a legal relationship in which to develop and grow through polygyny as opposed to her live alone, sleep around and/or be a mistress/girlfriend instead of being a co-wife? Which is fairer? Which is better? It is not automatically clear why being alone, single and unmarried is better or even fairer. Hence, the claim that the Shariah is unfair does not immediately follow.

Response 2:

- One of the underlying logic behind protestations against polygamy is as follows:

[P1] Men get to do X but women don't.

_____

[C3] *Therefore*, Shariah is unfair for allowing men to do X but not women.

- *Men as standard*: The hidden assumption behind this argument is that: *'whatever men are allowed to do, women should be allowed to do as well'*. This is a very bad argument. Two points why:

1. *Man is not the measure*: Should men be the standard for women? Should men be the yardstick by which to measure whether a woman has equality and fairness or not? No. Are women's progress to be measured according to how close they have come to men? No. Who made men the standard? Men. But why should this be the case? It shouldn't. The point is that neither men nor women are absolute standards for each other. So, equality predicated on how approximate women are to men is delusional and not objective at all. Standards, Muslim believe, are defined by Allah who is objective, unbiased and beyond human subjectivity.

2. *Impracticality*: Can we practically live by this principle of *'whatever men are allowed to do, women should be allowed to do it as well'*? Can we actually let everyone do the **SAME** things? Clearly not. Are students and teachers allowed to do the same thing? No. Are parents and children allowed to do the same thing? No. Are citizens and foreigners allowed to

do the same thing? No. Are members and non-members allowed to do the same thing? No. There are always some restrictions or reason why one person can do one thing and another cannot. Is this unfair? Do we call this unfairness or injustice? Why then in the case of the Shariah we call it unfairness?

- **Another problem:** *Contradictions*: if a woman is allowed to marry more than one man, she would have multiple husbands. According to Shariah, she could not *operationalise* that reality in that who will she obey when each husband demands to be with her because she has to obey her husband in the Shariah. How will she divide her Shariah duties between each husband? What if one husband does not allow her to leave the house but another demands she see him? Who should she obey? How can she build two homes consistently and effectively given her multiple duties and obligations? The entire context becomes an entangled and escapable mess. The entire Shariah legal structure will have to be altered and changed. In Islam, ***no-one*** has that right.

2.

'Sex, Slaves and Concubines!'

[P1] Islam allows sex with slave-girls.
[P2] But this is barbaric and unethical to women.

[C1] *Therefore*, the Shariah is barbaric and unethical to women.

Other arguments are:

1. It is to satisfy the lust of men.
2. It is a way of having multiple sexual partners.
3. It is a way of legalising a form of prostitution.

Response 1:

Context: **WAR**

- Slavery was not introduced by Islam but was in full existence when it came.
- Slavery was not regulated nor was it systematised before Islam.
- There was no assimilation model for slaves, war captives or prisoners of war (POW) in mainstream society before Islam.
- Historical context of POW and slaves is important to understand, as both were often inseparable realities – especially in relation to forming concubines.
- POW were treated inhumanely before Islam:

1) some POW were mutilated;
2) some POW were killed;
3) some POW were traded;
4) some POW were raped;
5) some POW were illegally ransomed and
6) some POW were forced into slavery.

- When Islam came it set in motion the mechanism by which to dissolve slavery as a practice such as:

1) through direct emancipation;
2) through emancipating a slave for expiation of a sin;
3) through the Caliph assigning Zakat revenues for emancipating slaves;
4) through slaves being contracted to freedom (*mukatab*), and many more ways.[254]

However, one reality and context that Islam restricted enslavement to was *war* or on-going conflict with enemies.

- In *jihad* scenarios, women POWs can become the possession of the Muslim soldier as military recompense through official permission of the *amir al-jihad* ('commander of jihad' which is usually the Caliph). This acquisition of the POW through official permission becomes a legal means of transfer that is in effect a substitute to a marriage ceremony:

Nevertheless, the wisdom underlying the permission granted by Shariat to copulate with a slave woman is as follows: The LEGAL possession that a Muslim receives over a slave woman from the "Ameerul-Mu'mineen" (the Islamic Head of State) gives him legal credence to have coition with the

---

[254] For which see the articles http://daralnicosia.wordpress.com/2012/06/20/slavery-and-islam-part-1-context/ and http://daralnicosia.wordpress.com/2012/06/23/slavery-and-islam-part-2-solutions/ for more details on this.

slave woman in his possession, just as the marriage ceremony gives him legal credence to have coition with his wife. In other words, this LEGAL POSSESSION is, in effect, a SUBSTITUTE of the MARRIAGE CEREMONY. A free woman cannot be 'possessed', bought or sold like other possessions; therefore Shariat instituted a 'marriage ceremony' in which affirmation and consent takes place, which gives a man the right to copulate with her. On the other hand, a slave girl can be possessed and even bought and sold, thus, this right of possession, substituting as a marriage ceremony, entitles the owner to copulate with her. A similar example can be found in the slaughtering of animals; that after a formal slaughtering process, in which the words, "Bismillahi Allahu Akbar" are recited, goats, cows, etc. become "Halaal" and lawful for consumption, whereas fish becomes "Halaal" merely through 'possession' which substitutes for the slaughtering. In other words, just as legal possession of a fish that has been fished out of the water, makes it Halaal for human consumption without the initiation of a formal slaughtering process; similarly legal possession of a slave woman made her Halaal for the purpose of coition with her owner without the initiation of a formal marriage ceremony...[255]

- This acquisition is a legal relationship in Shariah; as legal as a marriage. Below are the similarities and differences between a woman captive of war and a married woman:

---

[255] See http://askimam.org/public/question_detail/17032

Marriage	Woman POW
• Free.	• Slave.
• Marriage ceremony.	• Official allocation by Head of State.
• *Nafaqah.*	• *Nafaqah.*
• Only one husband.	• Only one owner/master.
• *'iddah* period.	• *Istibra'* period.
• Best treatment.	• Best treatment.
• Husband becomes unlawful to certain family members.	• Husband becomes unlawful to certain family members.
• Inheritance permitted.	• Inheritance permitted.
• Children born = free.	• Children born = free.

- How is the reality of POW or women captives to be dealt with? Islam's solution is to assimilate them into a society through a legal relationship with their owner and not left to become prostitutes, abused or maliciously traded like commodity.[256]

- **Question**: In today's world, how are POWs treated? **Answer** WWI prisoner killings, WWII POW massacres, mass concentration camps,

---

[256] See http://islamicresponse.blogspot.co.uk/2011/06/islam-on-slave-girlsconcubines.html

genocide, torture, rape, Guantanamo Bay, Abu Ghuraib, sex-trafficking, etc.

- If the aim of Islam is emancipation of slaves, if the aim of Islam is to assimilate existing slaves into mainstream society, if the aim of Islam is to offer a route for women captives to become a married woman and then freed after her marriage, if the aim of Islam is to grant rights to slaves and if the aim of Islam is to take responsibility of the very vulnerable then how can this be for the service of lust and sexual desire? How can this be an arrangement for merely servicing the male fantasy and sexual entrapment? The clear answer is **It isn't**.

Response 2:

- There is no 'find and grab' outcome, i.e. a solider arrests POWs and then they automatically become his; there is a process of law where POWs are handed over to the Islamic State after which the Caliph will decide to either: 1) free them; 2) return them to the enemy or 3) transfer ownership to the Muslim soldier. Often western myths are that women captives of war become a parcel or property for the soldiers and their delight. This is utterly false and pure propaganda. As outlined above, the social mechanism by which to integrate women POWs is through a legal relationship by which she will then become freed.[257]

---

[257] See for example: http://www.islamic-life.com/forums/quran-hadith-prophet-muhammad/islam-permit-muslim-men-rape-slave-girls-1832

Response 3:

- The laws pertaining to slaves and their high status as well as social mobility were what attracted non-Muslim slaves to Islam in droves.[258]

3.

'Hitting...'

[P1] Islam allows a husband to hit his wife
[P2] But this is barbaric and unethical to women.

[C1] *Therefore*, the Shariah is barbaric and unethical to women.

Response 1:[259]

- An Islamic marriage is about love, kindness, companionship, mercy and intimacy.

---

[258]
See
http://qa.sunnipath.com/issue_view.asp?HD=1&ID=1808&CATE=135
[259] See regarding this issue, some responses:

1. http://islamqa.org/hanafi/zamzam-academy/20486
2. http://sunniforum.net/showthread.php?t=594
3. http://spa.qibla.com/issue_view.asp?HD=12&ID=3119&CATE=10
4. http://spa.qibla.com/issue_view.asp?HD=11&ID=4758&CATE=121
5. http://spa.qibla.com/issue_view.asp?HD=11&ID=4863&CATE=121
6. http://spa.qibla.com/issue_view.asp?HD=12&ID=612&CATE=10

- The best Muslims are those who are best to their women.
- The Prophet hated that Muslims should hit their wives.[260]
- The Prophet never struck anyone in any context – except in *jihad*.[261]

Response 2:

- Media myths are regularly circulated about Islam and vulnerability of women under Shariah.
- Domestic violence and Islamic rulings is often equated together.
- Western moral superiority is asserted with a female liberation narrative.
- Some scholars have an incorrect way of handling the issue and deny what is explicit in the Qur'an.

---

[260] See *al-Mustadrak* of al-Hakim, 2:208 (#2775) and al-Bayhaqi, *al-Sunan al-Kubra*, 7:304: "...**the best of you do not hit their wives**..."

لن يضرب خياركم

[261] In the *Musannaf* of Ibn Abi Shybah, 8:368 (#25967) it states: "[...] and the Messenger of Allah (s) was the best of them and he never struck anyone..."

حَدَّثَنَا عَبْدَةُ ، عَنْ يَحْيَى بْنِ سَعِيدٍ، عَنِ الْقَاسِمِ، أَنَّ رِجَالاً نُهُوا عَنْ ضَرْبِ النِّسَاءِ، وَقِيلَ : لَنْ يَضْرِبَ خِيَارُكُمْ، قَالَ الْقَاسِمُ : وَكَانَ رَسُولُ اللهِ صلى الله عليه وسلم خَيْرَهُمْ كَانَ لاَ يَضْرِبُ...

Response 3:

- Disciplining one's wife is legally **allowed** in Islam. This is the bare legal ruling but there are details as with any Islamic ruling.

- **Firstly**, there is a process or series of stages the Qur'an lays down: [1] exhorting, advising, admonition; [2] refusal for marital intimacy and then [3] applying physical force or reprimanding by force.

- **Secondly**, context is important: authority sometimes may require force e.g. a government although cares for its citizens, sometimes uses force for their own good – (hence the need for police). Similarly, a husband has been given the authority (*wilayah*) or responsibility for ensuring the family remains on Islamic teachings. Sometimes, if matters become so extreme, <u>force may be necessary to prevent some evil taking place from the wife</u>. This is an allowance or legal permission but not an <u>open door policy</u>. There are conditions and pre-requisites to this permission or allowance for force such as:

1. When the wife is absolutely disobedient.
2. When the wife is absolutely depraved and lewd.
3. When the wife is extremely errant in her behaviour.
4. When the wife is recalcitrant.
5. When the wife is breaking her marital duties without reason.
6. When the wife is committing adultery.

- **Thirdly**, the following **is not** allowed:

  1. To hit for any old reason.
  2. To beat up the wife.[262]
  3. To beat the wife.[263]
  4. To hit the wife such that it leaves a mark.
  5. To hit such that it bruises.
  6. To hit such that it causes bleeding.
  7. To hit such that it breaks the bone.
  8. To strike the face.[264]
  9. To physically abuse the wife.
  10. To assault the wife.
  11. To hit in front of children.

- **Fourthly**, scholars have interpreted the striking (ضرب/*darb*) mentioned in the verse Q. 4:34-36 {...*and then strike them lightly*...} above to mean 'lightly' (غير مبرح/*ghayr mubarrih*) such as with a *siwak* (tooth stick) or tying a knot at the end of the shawl and not 'beating physically' because the latter is a form of oppression (*zulm*) and that is unlawful in Shariah.[265]

---

[262] Abu Dawud, *Sunan* (#2138).

[263] Abu Dawud, *Sunan* (#2139).

[264] Abu Dawud, *Sunan* (#4478).

[265] See al-Tabari, *al-Jami` al-Bayan*, 5:68:

حدثنا ابن حميد قال حدثنا حكام عن عمرو عن عطاء عن سعيد بن جبير : { واضربوهن } قال : ضربا غير مبرح

حدثنا ابن حميد قال حدثنا يحيى بن واضح قال أخبرنا أبو حمزة عن عطاء بن السائب عن سعيد بن جبير مثله

حدثنا ابن حميد قال حدثنا جرير عن مغيرة عن الشعبي قال : الضرب غير مبرح

حدثني المثنى قال حدثنا حبان بن موسى قال حدثنا ابن المبارك قال أخبرنا شريك عن عطاء بن السائب عن
سعيد بن جبير عن ابن عباس : { واضربوهن } قال : ضربا غير مبرح

حدثنا المثنى قال حدثنا أبو صالح قال حدثني معاوية عن علي بن أبي طلحة عن ابن عباس : { واهجروهن
في المضاجع واضربوهن } قال : تهجرها في المضجع فإن أقبلت وإلا فقد أذن الله لك أن تضربها ضربا غير
مبرح ولا تكسر لها عظما فإن أقبلت وإلا فقد حل لك منها الفدية

حدثنا الحسن بن يحيى قال أخبرنا عبد الرزاق قال أخبرنا معمر عن الحسن و قتادة في قوله : { واضربوهن
} قال : ضربا غير مبرح

وبه قال أخبرنا عبد الرزاق قال أخبرنا ابن جريج قال : قلت لعطاء : { واضربوهن } ؟ قال : ضربا غير مبرح

حدثنا بشر بن معاذ قال حدثنا يزيد بن زريع قال حدثنا سعيد عن قتادة : { واهجروهن في المضاجع
واضربوهن } قال : تهجرها في المضجع

فإن أبت عليك فاضربها ضربا غير مبرح أي : غير شائن

حدثنا المثنى قال حدثنا إسحق قال حدثنا ابن عيينة عن ابن جريج عن عطاء قال : قلت لابن عباس : ما
الضرب غير المبرح ؟ قال : السواك وشبهه يضربها به

حدثنا إبراهيم بن سعيد الجوهري قال حدثنا ابن عيينة عن ابن جريج عن عطاء قال قلت لابن عباس : ما
الضرب غير المبرح ؟ قال : بالسواك ونحوه

حدثنا المثنى قال حدثنا حبان بن موسى قال أخبرنا ابن المبارك قال أخبرنا ابن عيينة عن ابن جريج عن عطاء
قال : قال رسول الله صلى الله عليه وسلم في خطبته : ضربا غير مبرح قال : السواك ونحوه

حدثنا القاسم قال حدثنا الحسين قال حدثني حجاج قال : قال رسول الله صلى الله عليه وسلم : لا تهجروا
النساء إلا في المضاجع واضربوهن

ضربا غير مبرح يقول : غير مؤثر

حدثنا ابن وكيع قال حدثنا أبي عن إسرائيل عن جابر عن عطاء : { واضربوهن } قال : ضربا غير مبرح

حدثنا المثنى قال حدثنا حبان قال أخبرنا ابن المبارك قال حدثنا يحيى بن بشر عن عكرمة مثله

حدثنا محمد بن الحسين قال حدثنا أحمد بن مفضل قال حدثنا أسباط عن السدي : { واضربوهن } قال :
إن أقبلت في الهجران وإلا ضربها ضربا غير مبرح

حدثنا ابن وكيع قال حدثنا أبي عن موسى بن عبيدة عن محمد بن كعب قال : تهجر مضجعها ما رأيت أن
تنزع فإن لم تنزع ضربها ضربا غير مبرح

حدثني المثنى قال حدثنا عمرو بن عون قال حدثنا هشيم عن يونس عن الحسن : { واضربوهن } قال :
ضربا غير مبرح

حدثني المثنى قال حدثنا حبان قال حدثنا ابن المبارك قال أخبرنا عبد الوارث بن سعيد عن رجل عن الحسن
قال : ضربا غير مبرح غير مؤثر

Therefore, even with these basic responses, the force of the critic's arguments is lost. It cannot be claimed that Islam is irrational, illogical, inconsistent or contradictory; rather the Islamic injunctions are practical solutions and internally consistent. It is bias, misunderstanding, ignorance and propaganda that generates negative perceptions of these rulings.

[End]

Peace and Blessings be upon our Master,
Muhammad, the Chosen One;
Upon his family and Companions
And all who follow them.
Amin.

S. Z. Chowdhury.
Hampstead, London, 2009 (updated).

KEY REFERENCES

Arabic References:

Ibn 'Abidin, *Hashiyat Radd al-Muhtar 'ala 'l-Durr al-Mukhtar Sharh Tanwir al-Absar*, 7 vols. Beirut: Dar al-Ihya' al-Turath al-'Arabi, n.d.

——————— *Radd al-Muhtar 'ala 'l-Durr al-Mukhtar*, 8 vols. Karachi: H. M. S. Co., 1986.

al-Bahlawi, *Adillat al-Hanafiyya min al-Ahadith al-Nabawiyya 'ala 'l-Masa'il al-Fiqhiyya*, Damascus: Dar al-Qalam, 2007.

al-Maydani, *al-Lubab fi Sharh al-Kitab*, 4 vols. Karachi: Kutub Khana, n.d.

al-Haythami, *Majma' al-Zawa'id*, Cairo: Maktbat al-Qudsi, n.d.

——————— al-Haythami, *Majma' al-Zawa'id*, Beirut: Dar al-Kitab al-'Arabi, 1982.

Ibn al-Humam, *Fath al-Qadir li 'l-'Ajiz al-Faqir Sharh al-Hidaya*, 9 vols. Beirut: Dar al-Ihya' al-Turath al-'Arabi, 1997.

al-Kasani, *al-Bada'i' al-Sana'i' fi Tartib al-Shara'i'*, 6 vols. Beirut: Dar al-Ihya' al-Turath al-'Arabi, 2000.

al-Marghinani, *al-Hidaya Sharh Bidyat al-Mubtadi*, 4 vols. Beirut: Dar al-Kutub al-'Ilmiyya, 2000.

Mawlana Nizam, et al. *al-Fatawa al-Hindiyya*, 6 vols. Quetta: Maktaba Majdiyya, 1983.

─────── *al-Fatawa al-Hindiyya*, repr. Beirut: Dar al-Fikr, 1979.

─────── *al-Fatawa al-Hindiyya*, 6 vols. Beirut: Dar Ihya' Turath al-'Arabi, 1980.

al-Mawsili, *Kitab al-Ikhtiyar li-Ta'lil al-Mukhtar*, 5 vols. Cairo: Dar al-Ma'rifa, 2000.

al-Nabhani, Taqi al-Din, *al-Shakhsiyya al-Islamiyya*, 3 vols. Beirut: Dar al-Umma, 2003-2005.

─────── *Nizam al-Iqtisadi fi'l-Islam*, Beirut: Dar al-Umm, 2004.

al-Nadwi, S. al-*Fiqh al-Muyassar*, Karachi: Zam-Zam Publications, 2009.

Ibn Nujaym, *al-Bahr al-Ra'iq fi Sharh Kanz al-Daqa'iq*, 9 vols. Beirut: Dar al-Kutub al-'Ilmiyya, 1997.

Qudri Paşa, *al-Ahkam al-Shari'iyyah fi 'l-Ahwal al-Shakhsiyyah*, Cairo, 1924.

al-Qal'aji, M. et al, *Mu'jam al-Lughat al-Fuqaha'*, Beirut: Dar al-Nafa'is, 2000.

al-Quduri, *al-Mukhtasar* (English-Arabic text, trans. M. Kiani, London: Dar al-Taqwa, 2009).

al-Shurunbulali, *Nur al-Idah* (English-Arabic text, trans. W. Charkawi) n.p. 2004.

————— *Maraqi al-Falah Sharh Nur al-Idah*, Damascus: Maktabat al-'Ilm al-Hadith, 2001.

————— *Maraqi al-Falah Sharh Nur al-Idah*, Beirut: Dar al-Kutub al-'Ilmiyya, 1995.

————— *Imdad al-Fattah Sharh Nur al-Idah*, Damascus, n.p. 2001.

————— *Maraqi al-Sa'adat*, Beirut: Dar al-Kutub al-Lubnani, 1973 and English trans. by F. A. Khan, London: Whitethread Press, 2010.

————— *Sabil al-Falah fi Sharh Nur al-Idah*, Beirut: Dar al-Bayruti, n.d.

Usmani, M. T. *Takmilat Fath al-Mulhim*, 3 vols. Karachi: Maktabat-i Dar al-'Ulum, 1986-1987.

Urdu References:

Khan, Ahmed Reza. *al-'Ataya li-Nabawiyya fi' l-Fatawa al-Ridwiyya*, 6 vols. Mubarakpur: Sunni Darul Isha'at, 1981.

————— *al-'Ataya al-Nabawiyya fi' l-Fatawa al-Ridwiyya*, 12 vols. Faisalabad: Maktaba Nuriyya Ridwiyya.

Ludhianvi, Rashid Ahmad. *Ahsan al-Fatawa*, Karachi: H. M. S. Co, 1398–.

Usmani, 'Aziz al-Rahman. *'Aziz al-Fatawa*, Karachi: Darul Isha'at, n.d.

————— *'Aziz al-Fatawa*, 2 vols. Deoband Fatwa Department, n.d.

~Notes~

Made in the USA
Monee, IL
24 August 2022

12425492R00105